She's
THE BOSS

9 POWERFUL STEPS TO MASTERING LEADERSHIP FOR NEW FEMALE LEADERS
IN BUSINESS: HONE YOUR LEADERSHIP STYLE, COACH HIGH PERFORMING TEAMS AND OVERCOME IMPOSTER SYNDROME

Noelle Ingram

Table of Contents

Introduction

Leadership is a challenge. But in line with a lot of other things in life, while it's a challenge for both men and women, it's a whole lot more difficult for women.

One of the reasons it is so much harder for women than men is because women don't have the same amount of female role models they can look up to. Because men have always dominated those leadership roles, younger men moving up the career ladder have had male role models to look up to. As there are fewer women in leadership roles, women don't have the same opportunities which may contribute to the lack of confidence many women feel to follow their dreams of becoming a great leader. If not many women have done it before them, they may also think it is impossible for them.

That's why I decided to write a book on leadership specifically for women. It has all the stuff you need to know in order to become a great leader in the corporate world and in business, but it's written from a woman's point of view. Women often have less confidence than men, and they tend to communicate in different ways and use different styles of leadership, so I've discussed all these factors in the book.

I started off working in marketing after obtaining a degree at university in this subject. And then at thirty, I made a big career change which took some courage to do and joined the graduate scheme at one of the 'big four' accountancy firms. After eight years there, I moved to one of the other 'big four' and throughout this career I have been surrounded by inspiring leaders; most recently I've also taken on my own leadership role. I've learned all the lessons in this book the hard way!

I realized that if I wanted to progress, I'd need to hone my leadership skills. I started doing research, and reading very widely, and I also put myself forward for further training, and at times I found myself quite a long way from my comfort zone (that's part of learning leadership: if you're uncomfortable, that just means you're dealing with stuff at quite a personal level, and that can be a sign that you're succeeding in your quest).

I think people of my generation are quite lucky. Older women had a much harder time forging their careers. Companies didn't have gender equality policies, overtly sexist behavior (even harassment) was often tolerated, and there were far fewer women role models and mentors. Now, most companies are keen to offer a gender-neutral workplace, and many have mentoring schemes, with women at senior levels able to help those who are starting out or just moving up with their first or second promotion.

Look at women in the news. Kamala Harris is Vice-President of the US, Nancy Pelosi is Speaker of the House; Christine Lagarde is President of the European Central Bank, while Kristalina Georgieva runs the International Monetary Fund. Female Prime Ministers include New Zealand's Jacinda Ardern, Katrin Jakobsdottir of Iceland, Sheikh Hasina of Bangladesh, and Robinah Nabbaja of Uganda, Finland's Sanna Marin and Estonia's Kaja Kallas, while Ursula von der Leyen is President of the European Commission. You have a whole load of role models there!

In the corporate world, Mary Barra runs General Motors, Michele Buck runs The Hershey Company, Safra Catz runs Oracle Corporation, Vicki Hollub runs Occidental Petroleum and Lisa Su runs AMD. In Europe, Christel Heydemann runs France's biggest telecoms provider, and Marjan Rintel runs Dutch airline KLM; and women are catching up in Asia, where Ng Wei Wei is the first female CEO of UOB Malaysia, and Africa, where

Ruwayda Redfearn heads up Deloitte Africa.

So, women certainly can be leaders, even in sectors like construction, oil and gas, and technology, which have always been male dominated. But they still face some major challenges on the way there.

We'll start off by thinking about what it takes to be a good leader, and consider some of the stumbling blocks that can hinder women from progressing to the C-suite. We'll look at the careers of some of the most successful women; they each have unique qualities that have helped them to become great leaders.

If you're currently in a new leadership role, you will learn how to spot the differences between a manager and a leader and start to adopt those traits as you progress in your career. We'll look at how you can develop your own leadership style, use powerful female traits to your advantage, overcome imposter syndrome and build confidence in you and your team.

I will also share some practical tips such as managing your time and negotiating effectively.

We'll look at how you can develop a high performance team and assist your team members progress their careers. Most great leaders have helped the next generation of leaders to emerge; for instance, Napoleon created a whole school of great generals, and great investor Ben Graham educated other leading investors like Warren Buffett and John Templeton.

My motivation for writing this book was to help other women become great leaders. Chances are, if you're reading this book, you're either thinking of running your own business, progressing towards a Fortune 500 CEO role, or heading up a team or division in your current company. Or you might be a founding member of a social enterprise or running a charitable foundation.

But I hope that whatever you end up doing, you'll also be helping other women discover leadership – giving them confidence, mentoring and befriending them, perhaps even hiring and promoting them. Madeleine

Albright once said: "There is a special place in hell for women who don't help other women," but I prefer to think there is a special place in a paradise garden for sisters who help other sisters.

Let's get started!

Chapter One
WHAT DOES IT TAKES TO BE A GREAT LEADER?

What makes someone a successful leader? That's a very interesting question. Just think about it for a moment.

Here's a slightly different question: What makes _women_ successful leaders? Think about that for a while. Did you think of exactly the same qualities? Or did you think of different ones?

There's no single correct answer to this. In this chapter, we are going to explore some of the foundational skills that new leaders will need and then discuss some of the more general skills that will turn you into a great leader. No one is saying you need to be perfect at all of these just yet; some of these skills will be improved upon as you progress in your leadership role.

FOUNDATIONAL SKILLS NEEDED FOR NEW LEADERS

Communication – this isn't referring to how good you are at writing a letter or how great you are at presenting, but rather, how you engage with colleagues using both your head and your heart. Using your head ensures you get the practical outcome intended from the conversation, whereas using your heart ensures that you connect with people on a human level, using emotional intelligence. This core skill will be used throughout your career as a leader on many different occasions.

Coaching – helping and mentoring other people. A natural leader isn't in the game just for themselves, but will help others become leaders. In my current job, mentoring is very common throughout all levels of the organization. It's not a teacher–pupil relationship but a chance to get someone else's perspective and learn about their experiences.

I struggled with this earlier in my career, but through practice and pushing myself, I have improved in this area drastically.

Delegating – this is important so that you can focus on leading the business and others can focus on what they're good at to achieve results and build a happy team. This can be something many new leaders struggle with as they don't like to lose control. But it is something you should master as you move up the ranks in your career and work with more junior team members.

Managing conflict – this may feel uncomfortable at first because, let's face it, who wants to address conflict with friends and former peers? But it is a critical part of your job to recognize when you need to step into conflict and help to resolve it.

Driving change – according to 82% of board members and CEOs in the EY 2021 Global Board Risk Survey, market disruptions have become more frequent and impactful. As a leader you will almost inevitably be involved in managing transformation and you must understand how to turn resistance into commitment and inspire team members to take ownership of change. To keep pace with the rate of change, companies have begun to transform more frequently and EY believes that putting humans at the forefront can double your chances of success. According to the research there are six key drivers of successful change management; inspiring, leading, caring, empowering, collaborating and building. Inspire people; lead them through the change; care about their worries and anxieties;

empower them to be involved in the change process; encourage new ways of working through collaboration; build an infrastructure for transformation.

Inclusion – great leadership is inclusive and must be built into the core skills you practice daily. Many companies now incorporate diversity and inclusion values as part of their strategy.

Now let's look at some of the more general qualities that you need to become a great leader:

- Confidence in your ability to follow through right to the end; persistence. Famously, JK Rowling received twelve rejection letters before, at long last, Bloomsbury decided to publish *Harry Potter.*

- Willingness to step out of your comfort zone. The comfort zone can be a prison: so many women rise to the top of a division like finance or human resources, but they don't move up from there to CEO. Stepping outside your comfort zone is where all the magic happens and you achieve great things.

- Being able to get buy-in from your team to work towards a common goal. You'll need to be persuasive, but you'll also need a clear sense of that goal and the ability to listen to people as they think about what it means for them.

- Holding yourself and others accountable. You can't afford to be a 'Queen Bee' boss who only holds others to account. If you miss a target or make a mistake, fess up. Being honest with your team will make them honest with you in return.

- Being an innovator and encouraging innovation in your team (pianist Vladimir Horowitz said: "Always there should be a little mistake here and there – I am for it. The people who don't do mistakes are cold like ice. It takes risk to make a mistake. If you don't take risks, you are boring").

- Seeing failure as an opportunity to learn rather than letting it set you back. Sometimes you may find your failures all point to a weakness you can do something about, such as making plans that are too ambitious or failing to examine the finances closely enough, and that just says you need training in those aspects. Encourage no-blame post-mortems, thinking about what your team could have done differently and what the result might have been.

- Encouraging creative thinking. 'Outside the box' is a bit of a buzz phrase, but in a way, it's useful: we often box ourselves in by describing our objectives in a way that limits our ability to respond.

- Taking a long-term view. A war leader, for instance, can't just fight one battle; they have to see the whole campaign and how each battle achieves a vital objective. If you don't take a long-term view, you may win the battle but lose the war.

- Keeping on growing. We often believe that the leader is the one who's finished their learning and got to the top. In fact, if they don't continue learning, they will not stay there long. Focus on self-development and self-critique – set an example to your team and allow them to learn and grow.

- Knowing your worth. This is something women have particular issues with! Real leaders know they are valuable and have a keen idea of their own strengths, even if they have to persevere against opposition. Self-confidence and self-esteem aren't given, but they can be learned.

- Picking the right battles. If you want to improve your organization's processes, wait for the right opportunity to change things rather than keeping up a low-level rumble of discontent. If you can, suggest solutions rather than just complaining.

- Respecting others. There's a particular kind of macho management approach that asserts that a leader looks bigger if they can make everyone else look small. There are also the sneaky people who try to steal the credit from other people. You're not going to get great performance from people who feel you're taken credit for their ideas, denigrated them, or simply think you don't respect them. Do that, and you're not a leader but an oppressor.

- Building relationships with peers. If you're leading one of several teams, know the other leaders and be interested in what problems they've encountered and how they're dealing with them. Building those relationships, even if difficult, will help you as you move towards leadership and will ensure you have broad-based support for your aspirations.

- Recognizing what you want and being bold enough to go after it. I remember in my last job, I really wanted a particular secondment to a project team abroad to get some cross-cultural experience. I hoped my boss would realize I wanted the opportunity. But when I rather hesitantly suggested: "I thought this job would really broaden my horizons," he said he hadn't thought I was interested in working overseas (male bosses often seem not to realize that women can be ambitious. A friend got asked what her partner would think if she got promoted... I can't imagine a man being asked that!).

- Seeking out opportunities. It can be easy to coast in a job and do it well, but don't just let yourself get carried along. Look for ways to do a bit more or something different – help train a new graduate, with a school's outreach program, with colleagues you know are struggling with a deadline.

- Being consistent. You need to have a central approach to create a consistent leadership language and culture. In other words, the messages you deliver, your underlying principles and behaviors must align with the organizational culture.

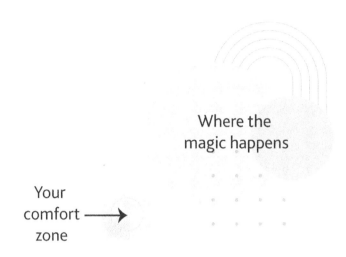

Where the
magic happens

Your
comfort ⟶
zone

These are all aspects of leadership. But let's see if we can come up with something a bit more concise. What about …

The four Cs of leadership

Character

You may have read the word 'character' and thought that this means great leaders are born, not made. But that's not quite the case. Character isn't innate; it is *formed* by your own experiences and your own decisions.

You form your own character by being honest with and about yourself. You might know that particular temptations are dangerous, for instance, so why those particular ones? You may have weaknesses, but you become stronger by understanding and addressing them. For instance, you may be someone who often seeks approval and wants to be liked. But nonetheless, you may decide to be brave and risk disapproval when you're backing an unpopular cause.

I once was walking in the countryside and saw a child almost crying with fear. They were about to cross a railway sleeper laid across a stream. It didn't look very safe to me, and if I had been a tiny six-year-old, I would have been scared, too. They looked at the perilous bridge for a long time. And then, quite firmly, they walked over. That's character. Being afraid is okay; but admitting your fear and then overcoming it, that's character.

You also need to understand what you're passionate about, what you're trying to achieve. It may be the environment (Greta Thunberg is clear about that). It may be pushing cloud computing in new directions, as far as you can. Most of the people I know who do well at anything have a real passion for one particular thing, and they use that as their compass and as their motivation as well.

A big question you need to ask is: Do you inspire respect? Do people trust you? If the answer is "no," or "sometimes," then you need to do some hard thinking, because to be a leader, you have to inspire trust. What weaknesses can you address that will make that answer "yes"? Perhaps to gain respect, you just have to work on holding in your sense of humor, which tends to break out at all the wrong times. Perhaps to gain trust, you need to make eye contact with people instead of looking down. Or it might be more difficult; perhaps you need to tame your 'hard negotiator' and learn to be more forgiving.

You might also ask: What strengths do you have that people can rely on? Are you a good shoulder to cry on? Are you a motivator and enthusiast, a generator of great ideas or slogans, or a problem-solver who can always manage to find an emergency fix? Those strengths are the ones you'll rely on in your career, so make sure you know them.

Competence

One of the worst experiences I've had in my career is working for someone who thought he knew everything. He decided the marketing plan, he decided the business plan, he ran the finances, and he believed he was a real Mr Motivator (his motivation technique consisted of sneaking up on people in the office and suddenly asking them "Are you happy?"). I didn't stay long – nor did anyone else. Staff turnover was practically 100% a year.

Know your competences. For instance, if you understand computer networks and cybersecurity, then ensure that you make your contribution to any conversation or meeting that has a cybersecurity angle. If you don't understand those issues, then recognize the fact and get someone on your team who does, or ask for advice from someone else. Form strong partnerships with people who have competences that you don't and collaborate with them. And while you may never become an expert on their particular areas of competence, try to learn enough from them that you know when you need to call for help.

Keep learning. If you have a hard time understanding finance, and that's the main thing standing between you and excelling in your role, then you need to get some basic finance training. You don't need an accountancy qualification, but you need to get yourself on a finance course for management or grab some textbooks and put in a few weekends of hard work. And of course, there's nothing stopping you asking one of your finance colleagues for a bit of help, if you've already built that relationship.

Collaboration

Because you know your competences, you also know what competences you'll need to bring on board to collaborate with other teams. They may involve specific areas like finance, IT or marketing skills, or they may be soft skills, even just a counterbalance to your own. For instance, if you're the visionary, find someone who can bring you down to earth and keep your feet on the ground. A lot of visionary CEOs have a CFO they can rely on to ground them firmly in the business of meeting their budgets. If you're good with engineering but less good with people, find a couple of colleagues you trust who can warn you if you're alienating team members or not supporting them enough.

Courage

I'll never forget the time I was asked to manage a corporate weekend. The idea was to get all the eighty people in our division away for the weekend and have a mix of presentations about the business with some fun activities like off-road driving.

We'd pretty nearly got the schedule organized when I realized my team had gone very quiet. Then May spoke up – a small girl who rarely said much, but we all knew that when she did, it was important.

"You know the off-road driving?" she said.

"Yes," I replied. "I think that's going to be great fun. It'll get us all out in the open air, away from the presentations, give us a chance to relax."

"Well, that's a nice idea. But... a third of the people coming on the weekend don't actually have driving licences. They're going to feel left out."

I'm really glad she spoke up. I had no idea – I thought everyone could drive (I'm a country girl; where I grew up, everyone gets their first car at eighteen). So instead, we organized a treasure hunt around the grounds of the hotel, which everyone enjoyed.

That was courage. May was really shy and lacking in confidence, and she was the youngest member of the team, but she knew I was making a big mistake and she knew she had to say something. From that day, she had my respect and I made a point of asking for her to work on project teams I headed up. Later on, she took a couple of courses for women in management and became much more confident; she's just decided to take up a job offer running her own team.

Courage isn't physical bravery. It's being willing to say something unpopular, or to stick to your convictions and push change forward despite resistance from some areas of the organization.

It can take courage to say directly to someone that you're having to let them go. It's interesting how many tech sector CEOs don't have that courage, and resort to using email or WhatsApp or a Zoom meeting to do it.

Traits of a great leader

I want to dig down a little more into the traits of great leaders, and the way they behave. Let's put some flesh on the bones. I have included these so that you can not only start to think about what it takes to be a great leader but also so that you can start to incorporate some of these into your role. The more you practice something, the more it will feel second nature.

Great leaders share their vision

Great leaders have a vision, and they know how to share it with others. That might be through great oratory and public speeches, or just through showing it quietly again and again in the way they behave. For instance, the Dalai Lama both shares his values of compassion and calm, and demonstrates them in his daily life and the way he displays empathy with everyone he meets. Marcus Rashford, England footballer, has been a huge opinion leader with his fight for kids from deprived backgrounds to get free school meals, and one reason for this is the way he speaks about his own background and his obvious commitment to his family and his home area. You can have a great vision, but unless you can help your team relate that to their daily work, you're better off as an inventor, a novelist or a painter rather than a leader.

'Leader' and 'boss' are two different things, and it's vision that is one of the big differences. So is leading by example. If a CEO is trying to save 20% costs across the organization, buying a new corporate jet is not a good look.

Their vision may be a personal one, but obviously it needs to relate to the vision of the organization they work for. Can they inspire others to understand and follow that vision too? Can they share the vision?

A leader will think about their organization and ask the question: "What do we want to be in the future?"

The answer might be, for example: "The best artisan bakery and coffee roaster in town," or it might be "The dominant computer operating system in the world."

Let's look at the answers from a few real-world companies:

- Amazon – "To be Earth's most customer-centric company, where customers can find and discover anything they might want to buy online."

- Apple – "We believe that we are on the face of the earth to make great products and that's not changing."
- Ben and Jerry's – "Making the best possible ice cream, in the nicest possible way."

Having a great vision means you can set great goals – tangible, measurable, specific goals and deadlines that members of your team can work on – while understanding their relation to the vision. Goals must be ambitious but realistic.

Bad leadership drops the vision and starts to focus exclusively on the goals. For instance, if the police are not driven by a vision of protecting society and preventing crime, but simply by a target number of arrests, they will pursue easy-to-prove small nuisances and put less effort into investigating serious crime. Doctors who have targets for certain tests or procedures may focus on meeting those rather than serving their patients' best interests.

Integrity

Leaders have their own clear values. They might be controversial; some activist shareholders and hedge fund managers have quite Darwinist-sounding views on making sure only the fittest companies survive. However, their values are clear and they do act in accordance with them; they're willing to be judged on their record.

Leaders make a promise and keep it; they don't look to the small print for a get-out clause. They're direct and honest with people; if they feel that you let them down, they'll tell you, rather than bearing a grudge or talking about you behind their back.

If they're not transparent, they're not a leader.

Effective Communication

We already touched on this as a foundational skill of leadership, about the importance of connecting at a human level. Great leaders are clear, concise, and when needed, tactful (I highly recommend the British TV series 'Yes, Minister' for a masterclass in a particular type of communication skills, though I don't recommend you follow Sir Humphrey's example). They share information with everyone who needs it, presenting it in such a way that it can be used most effectively.

Great leaders also remember that communication is a two-way process. They ask intelligent questions but are also willing to ask ones that may seem stupid. They solicit input and know how to get people to talk freely. They also know how to clarify what's said in order to avoid misunderstandings ("Is everyone clear about what 'data cleansing' actually means?").

Effective communication also involves engaging your audience. If you do all the things I've already mentioned but you bore people, if you can't communicate some energy and enthusiasm or at least determination, then you're talking but not leading.

Decisiveness

Leaders often have to make a decision without having all the information, and may have to do it very quickly. For instance, a crisis situation such as a fire at a factory or a sudden computer outage demands fast action.

Part of decisiveness is being able to think fast about what you need to achieve and the likely consequences of different courses of action. You may also need to be able to identify very quickly the one or two pieces of information that you really do need – for instance, in the case of a fire, whether there's anyone in the factory, and whether there's any hazardous material in the factory.

Having made your decision, stick to it; be consistent. Flip-flopping is not leadership. Take responsibility; make sure the decision is followed through.

Recognizing success

Leaders value their people and what they do. Their recognition of success isn't always formal, but it's always genuine. Leaders understand what that success means to the team member – it may be small in terms of the overall effort, but a huge achievement for that individual.

A heartfelt "thank you" said privately as you're all packing up after a meeting can mean more to a team member than any number of 'X of the Month' awards. Do it in person if you can – face to face, by phone, or by Zoom can be used too. And do it the way the person will appreciate; if you know one of your team members is shy, don't call them up on stage at a big conference.

Understanding what went into the job, or asking: "How did you get that result? How difficult was it? Were you worried?" can make a huge impact. Celebrating even small successes is the sign of leadership. And celebrate success *before* you start to critique. Constructive feedback comes best sandwiched with appreciation at both ends.

Empowering others
Great leaders empower others. They don't control them.

Have you ever worked for a boss who's a micromanager? I have. You always feel under pressure, and you can't do things your way and in your time. No wonder teams don't give their best in that environment. In many ways, this kind of management is left over from the days of industrial standardization when 'managers' were given all the responsibility and 'workers' just had to do what they were told. In today's service and knowledge economy, it's no longer a useful way to manage people.

Great leaders invest time and effort in making sure everyone understands the vision, the goals, and the deadlines that need to be achieved. Then they give their people responsibility for managing their work and the authority to use the resources they need. They encourage creativity and innovation. In return, they get a team that will deliver and that doesn't need to be 'managed.' Questions are at the heart of empowerment. A great leader asks questions so that their employees can think deeply and come to a solution on their own. A great leader asks questions to grow and develop their mindset alongside their colleagues. The more questions you ask, the better you will become at it and the deeper the team will think.

Motivation

Leaders motivate and inspire, rather than command and control. That motivation comes from within: they're passionate about what they're trying to achieve, and that enthusiasm communicates itself to others.

They understand the emotional and personal side of motivation, too. They will invest time in understanding the other members of their team and what's important for them in terms of their jobs, but also personally. In what areas are they strong and confident? Where might they need extra resources or training? What makes them feel proud of their work?

If you have real enthusiasm, and you know your team, you'll easily be able to motivate them.

Confidence

A leader is confident – or at least manages to look it. Even if a leader is making a desperate gamble, as battle leaders sometimes have to do, once the decision has been made, they won't look back; they'll carry out the mission as if they know they will win.

Leaders need to believe they can achieve their goals and vision. You'll need to believe in yourself and in your mission, to know your strengths and be confident about them. This isn't about 'fake it to make it,' but is about being grounded and being prepared to trust your judgment when you have thought things through. It's about the ability to take risks, be it a difficult project, a big change in the way your department works, taking on a new study course or a new job.

If you believe in yourself, others will believe in you. It all starts with you; that's what makes you a leader.

Accountability

Great leaders have integrity and they hold themselves accountable for their actions. When they make a mistake, they admit it. Great leaders will apologize to team members if they have misjudged them; they will make amends if they failed to recognize an individual's contribution.

Being accountable builds trust, because the team can see that their leader is honest enough not to blame them for their own problems. They can also see that their leader is big enough to take it on the chin.

Commitment to learning

Real leaders are committed to their teams' development. Napoleon said: "Every soldier of France carries a field marshal's baton in his knapsack." Promotion in his army was on merit, and his men knew it. Granted, most of them learned their trade in battle rather than at school, but a commitment to team members' career progression and lifelong learning is a key motivator.

If you're a real leader, you're creating the next generation of leaders.

Knowing they can't do it all

Great leaders are like orchestral conductors: they don't have to play any of the instruments, but they're the person who puts the sound together and creates the music. They know they can't do everything and so they delegate. Their biggest impact comes through deciding what *not* to do and what *not* to decide – what they can leave to others to do. That frees them up to do the really important things that only they can do. One of the leaders in my team is great at this: she lets the team members get on with their work, while she does the things that are important to her role, such as forming the values and goals of the organization and getting involved with any high-risk client projects with more senior clients.

Understanding people dynamics

Great leaders understand other people's agendas and sensitivities and know how to reconcile these to their overall vision. For instance, a visionary leader wanting to launch a new product will know that finance is unlikely to back her ideas unless she comes up with a robust business plan.

But this isn't 'playing office politics.' It's important to understand people dynamics so that you don't have to compromise your overall vision and objectives. Poor leaders play office politics as a game; great leaders see when other people are playing politics and know how to steer around them.

Moving their focus

Great leaders can shift focus quickly from the tiniest detail up to the overall plan, or anywhere in between. Like good film directors, they can zoom in and out, use close-ups or tracking shots or panoramic lenses.

Just seeing the big picture isn't enough. Sometimes, a tiny detail makes a huge difference, but it needs to be seen in terms of the overall plan. Switching between different perspectives is the sign of a leader. Switching between different time perspectives is important, too: that new development in your industry that's too small and niche and expensive to invest in right now might loom larger in four or five years' time.

Focusing on what's important

Great leaders focus on what's important. That means having just one or two priorities, not chasing too many different objectives. They are clear about where the best places to use their energy and resources are.

Solving problems

A good leader is prepared for obstacles to arise. Some people are great at enthusiasm and cheerleading, but when they hit an obstacle, they don't have what it takes to keep the team together. Problem-solving is a key part of the leader's kit.

It starts with trying to foresee problems and explain any difficulties to the team up front. It continues with keeping a positive attitude, providing a source of energy and enthusiasm to pick up a team that's experienced a set-back, and get them on their feet again. It may involve sharing problems, asking for input and being ready to think seriously, even about proposals that at first seem strange or mad.

If your first reaction to a setback is to look for someone to blame, you're not a leader.

Encouraging innovation

Encouraging creativity and innovation is one of the most important things a leader can do. The world used to be full of bosses who told their employees: "You're not paid to think." Needless to say, staff soon learned not to bother with suggestions for improvements or new products. But such firms made it through to the 1980s and even 1990s just by doing things the way they always had. They're rapidly dying out now, though.

Why? Because the world is changing and it's also becoming more complex. Companies that take their competitive environment for granted die out quickly. Eastman Kodak dominated the world of film, didn't see the threat coming from digital cameras and smartphones, and was bankrupt by 2012. Fujifilm, its counterpart in Japan, on the other hand, diversified, built up a strong digital camera business and other diversifications, and ran its film division as a cash cow, squeezing money out of it.

Encouraging creativity isn't just about activities like brainstorming. It's about being creative yourself, encouraging team members to come up with ideas, and thinking widely about different approaches to responding to disruptive change. Your clarity of purpose needs to come from your vision, not from "the way we've always done things." Root your team in a strong vision and mutual self-respect, and you've already gone a long way towards making your team an innovative one.

Long-term vision

Some teams spend the vast majority of their time fire-fighting and concentrating on short-term goals. They are almost always the teams that underperform. On the other hand, businesses that are doing well tend to spend as much as 80% of their time taking actions that will benefit them in the long term, while short-term management takes just a fifth of their time.

The difficulty, of course, is that when the going gets tough and there's a short-term problem to be solved, most leaders and most teams tip back into firefighting mode. That happened to many companies during the Covid pandemic. Some airlines laid off so many staff that when demand came back, they couldn't cope. On the other hand, nimble brew-pubs pivoted from hospitality to delivery businesses, keeping their beer lines working even though they couldn't host on-premises customers.

Keeping the long-term in view meant planning for the pandemic as, on most expectations, a one-to-three-year disruption, and thinking where the business ought to be at the end of that period. By referring to that vision, the business should be able to navigate short- and medium-term turbulence successfully. My company kept all staff on during the pandemic and it has paid off long-term: we are now stronger than ever and hiring more people to help build our teams.

Seeing failures as opportunities

Irish playwright Samuel Beckett is often seen as a rather depressing writer, but he said one thing that is both realistic and inspiring: "Ever tried? Ever failed? No matter. Try again. Fail again. Fail better."

We learn by failure. Remember learning to walk, or to ride a bicycle? If we defined our early experience as toddlers in terms of *failing* to walk, we would be right, but we'd be ignoring the fact that eventually, we get past that stage, and get better at standing on our own feet, till walking is perfectly normal and we don't even have to think about it.

Failure is good for us as long as we don't let it define us. Every time we mess up, we learn. Every time we have to struggle, we learn. Failure forces us to grow and it makes us resilient – like toddlers learning to bounce back and get back on their feet when they fall over. So, you should see struggle and potential failure as opportunities for your own personal growth, and for the growth of your team's abilities.

Remember, too, that sometimes failures create new products. In France, there's a well-known candy called 'Bêtises de Cambrai' – 'Cambrai mistakes.' An apprentice toffee maker forgot to look after the boiling pot, and the candy cooked too hard. Total failure... Or total success. The apprentice had invented a new boiled sweet, which now sells 400 tons a year.

Self-development

Leaders are made, not born. You can become a leader, and you can become a better leader, as long as you're prepared to work on it. We already touched on this earlier, but self-improvement isn't just about doing training courses or getting qualifications; it's about becoming a better person. For instance, all leaders have weaknesses that they need to work on, such as a short temper, getting stressed too easily, or sticking to their comfort zone.

To be a great leader, you need to work on yourself. Prioritize the things that are stopping you achieving your potential. And let your team see that you're doing it; encourage team members to do the same.

Building relationships and networks

Good leaders know many people they can call on for help, a second opinion, or a shoulder to cry on. They know people at different levels and with different skills and from different backgrounds. It gives them a rich tapestry of support.

'Networking' is a bit of a buzzword for some people, so you might want to think more in terms of establishing and maintaining good relationships, or good connections. Take time to get to know people in other parts of your organization. For instance, if you have to get a finance sign-off for one of your projects, don't treat it as a one-off requirement, but spend a bit of time getting to know the finance team. If another team appeals for help, don't think of it as a resource drain, but as a chance to find new allies.

Outside your organization, look for opportunities to meet people; professional associations, conferences, events, or secondments. If you are not a 'networky' kind of person, offer to give a speech or sit on a committee, to contribute to newsletters, or to find some other task that will let you meet other people while taking part. Get to know people at supplier or client companies, too. Their input will be very useful to you in building up a picture of the competitive environment you're working in.

Stay in touch with people who have mentored you, or who you've mentored, or worked with or for, if they move on to another part of your organization or to work somewhere else.

At the start of your career, networking might be about finding job opportunities. But later on, it's more about having plenty of people that you can ask for advice, recruit to a project team, or check out a joint venture idea with.

Diversity and inclusiveness

Diversity is *not* just 'political correctness.' It's actually a positive value. For instance, when you look at nature, you see that a polyculture – different species of plants growing together – is much stronger and more resistant to disease than a monoculture like a cornfield. In the same way, a team that's composed of people from different backgrounds, male and female, from different races and perhaps with different beliefs, can be stronger than a team recruited exclusively from a single type of individual.

One of the foundational skills of a great leader is to create a culture of inclusiveness. True inclusiveness means accepting people for what they are and using their particular strengths within the team. You may have someone on the team who has particular ways of thinking around problems and sometimes comes up with startlingly good but unexpected answers (I used to work with a Star Trek fan who would occasionally criticize my weaker ideas by saying simply, "Not logical, captain!"). You may have quiet people and more vocal people, task-orientated people and people who are more into processes or who are people-orientated. Sometimes you'll need to adjust your own attitudes a little: people from some cultures are very loath to speak out, while some working-class youngsters are used to robust give and take.

Inclusiveness can find the right place for everyone, but you do have to make an effort to get there. And I feel, very much, that pursuing inclusiveness is the right thing for me to do as a woman, because I have benefited from the corporate world opening up to women, and I want to continue that inclusivity.

TRAITS OF A GREAT LEADER

- Are great communicators
- Are able to coach others
- Delegating successfully
- Are able to manage conflict
- Drive change
- Are inclusive
- Have the confidence to follow through
- Step out of their comfort zone
- Are able to get buy in from the team
- Hold themselves and others accountable
- Are innovative and encourage innovation
- See failure as an opportunity to learn
- Encourage creative thinking
- Take a long term view
- Keep on growing
- Know their worth
- Pick the right battles
- Respect others
- Build relationships with peers
- Recognize what they want and are bold enough to go after it
- Seek out opportunities
- Are consistent
- Form their own character

- Know their competencies
- Collaborate with others
- Have courage
- Share their vision
- Have integrity
- Effectively communicate
- Are decisive
- Recognize success in others
- Empower others
- Motivate others
- Are accountable for their actions
- Commit to learning
- Show confidence
- Know they can't do it all
- Understand people dynamics
- Quickly move their focus
- Focus on what's important
- Are able to solve problems
- Encourage innovation
- Have a long-term vision
- See failure as an opportunity
- Practice self-development
- Build relationships and networks
- Promote diversity and inclusiveness

Chapter Two
OVERCOMING THE STUMBLING BLOCKS FOR FEMALE LEADERS

t's not easy becoming a leader, but there are particular difficulties facing women who want to move up to leadership. Often women feel they're in a catch-22 situation: if they display feminine behavior, they won't be seen as leaders, but if they try to be 'one of the boys,' they'll be seen as fakes.

So, in this chapter, I'm going to uncover some of the stumbling blocks facing women specifically, and suggest how you can avoid the pitfalls. I am going to start with the differences in confidence between men and women as this can be one of the main ways that can hold women back from taking the opportunity for leadership roles or becoming a great leader.

Differences in confidence between men and women

Self-confidence is an important part of leadership, but research shows that women generally have much less self-confidence than men. Men are more likely to be over-confident, in fact, which is really a weakness. As Steven Smith says: "The great irony is that women have more of the natural traits of real confidence than men. Typically speaking, men have a propensity to be overconfident, leaving them irrelevant and exposed to failure more often than they should be."

Even successful women, who look confident to others, may not have as much self-confidence as it appears. They may undervalue their own abilities, which can cause them to forgo opportunities for learning or promotion. Lower confidence may also prevent women asking for promotion or pay raises. A 2011 UK study by the Institute of Leadership and Management showed that only a third of male managers reported self-doubt, whereas half the women said they doubted themselves.

Men will often apply for a job where they don't quite fulfil the requirements but expect to be able to learn on the job. Women will often *not* apply for a job for which they're fully qualified, worrying that they are not quite experienced enough. Men negotiate their salaries four times more often than women – and women ask for a third less money, even when they negotiate (see Linda Babcock's book *Women Don't Ask* for the numbers).

While women have made huge progress, the higher up you go, the less progress has been made. In the US, women now get more college and graduate degrees than men and are closing the gap in middle management. But right at the top, men are still getting the jobs. The 'glass ceiling' is real.

And even those women who have made it right into the C-suite admit to sometimes wondering if they are frauds – something male execs rarely do. Sometimes they consider they've just been 'lucky' in their careers (we'll talk about imposter syndrome later, with some good advice for how to tackle it).

The honest truth? In experiments by psychologist Brenda Major at UC Santa Barbara, men and women were asked how they thought they would perform on a variety of tasks. Men predicted better outcomes than women. She then asked them to do the tasks. The actual outcomes were the same for both men and women. Faced with any task, men tend to overestimate their performance, while women underestimate – but in fact, when you look at their performance in reality, both perform exactly the same.

'Womenomics' is an interesting new discipline. The word was first used by Kathy Mitsui, managing director of Goldman Sachs Japan, who believes greater female engagement in the workforce could increase the size of Japan's economy by 14%. Womenomics involves looking at why women don't pursue their careers and removing roadblocks; support for women returning to work after maternity leave, for instance, is largely missing in Japan. The government of Jordan has also adopted womenomics as a strategy. In Jordan, women have achieved equality in education, but that hasn't transferred to the world of work; that's partly due to 'glass ceilings' but also to the way many textbooks portray women in the limited roles of mother or teacher, and don't show women as leaders. That's a different roadblock – the lack of role models and positive examples.

If women can effect such a huge change economically, then why isn't it happening? Of course, there are still some roadblocks even in the West, like affordable childcare, but the confidence gap is another big reason.

You may not feel really confident yet, but it's worth knowing the things that will make you *look* confident. Relatively expansive body language is important; for instance, an open stance doesn't just suggest you're confident, but also suggests you are open and willing to engage with others positively. Walk as if you know where you're going, and people will assume that you do.

One of the things Margaret Thatcher worked a lot on during her political career was her voice. Having a deeper voice is connected with confidence and authority, and calm speech patterns also suggest *gravitas*, the quality of being serious and authoritative. That's obviously something that will take women a while to develop. It does affect men too – think of the way men with high-pitched voices are often considered effeminate or comic.

A big problem for many women is that they assume when things get tough, it's personal – that they must have done something wrong, or be failing. In fact, if things get tough, it's probably because they *are* tough. If your division is losing sales in the middle of a recession, it's not you, it's the economy that's failing.

Don't brood on negative experiences or failures. If you get negative feedback for your team or product, try not to take it personally. Consider it as information, not necessarily right or wrong but just data that you can think about and perhaps use to your advantage.

Don't second-guess yourself. If you really believe that a course of action is the right one to take, then take it. And put yourself forward for different challenge. Action breeds confidence, which is one reason people who succeed at one thing (for instance, sport at school) often end up being successful in other ways.

Other stumbling blocks women face in their quest to be great leaders

Let's take a look specifically at the other stumbling blocks facing women – particular challenges that men don't have to face. For instance, equality in the workplace really hasn't arrived, even though many enterprises are trying hard to make it happen. A man may find he's given plenty of opportunities to shine – perhaps a secondment abroad, a high-profile project, or representing the business at a conference. Women often don't get asked, so make sure you stick your hand up, make your claim, and keep asking for the experiences and challenges that you want to take on.

The problem comes from our history; there is a well-established culture where men have held most of the top positions. People tend to pass the baton down to people similar to them, people they can relate to – other men! Men may feel that they are familiar with the skills and abilities of other men and may misunderstand the capabilities of women. Don't get me wrong, women have played a big part in business for a long time now but their roles tend to be lower down the ranks, more of the background roles in an organization.

I already talked about confidence, but women often find they're on the receiving end of some very hard knocks. That's particularly the case for women working in a male-dominated environment. I remember giving a high-level speech once, and most of the feedback was excellent, but one person simply wrote: "That pink shirt was a mistake." I can't imagine a man would have received that kind of feedback. It was very personal, so it hurt, but I had to get past it. Men don't usually get such personal abuse.

A big stumbling block for many women is relaunching themselves after maternity leave or after taking time off to start a family. Some, also, take time to care for aged parents; even if they don't stop working, they deprioritize work for a while. Relaunching your career is a challenge, because it means rebuilding your contacts and network, catching up on changes in the market or in technology, and making it clear that you're committed to moving upwards. However, it can be done. And if you see other women relaunching themselves, give them some help – you might not have gone 'mommy track' yourself, but you're helping your sisters move forward.

Many women may be single parents and once they get home, they need to take care of the house and the children so they don't have the same time investment men may have to put into their work and careers. Even in traditional families where there are two parents, women still tend to do the bulk of the housework and caring for the kids, running them to football matches or dance classes. Leadership roles require a lot of time and attention to the role, and this can make women unwilling or unable to pursue more senior roles within their organization.

Women find it harder to speak up. You may be a senior manager, but if you just sit at the table without saying anything, you can't lead. Men will often 'talk through' women, and their leadership style often doesn't involve trying to elicit comments from other team members, so you may need to speak up quite loudly. Don't get rattled if you are interrupted, but don't let men get away with it – just say: "There's one more thing to mention," or "Wait a minute, I have a couple more points to make." Give advice, share your perspective to shape policy, and ensure that you are given due respect.

Women can be seen as emotional and, therefore 'less effective' leaders. They generally express emotions more and are assumed to be more emotional. This can often be seen negatively; women can be seen as irrational or demanding. These are stereotypes that women are often judged on; many may find these tough to overcome in their quest to be a leader.

The workplace also expects less from women. Women have to work harder for leadership roles to prove themselves. Less is expected of them if they're not expected to become leaders. For example, women with children are expected to work fewer hours. Still, even women with no children are assumed to want children in the future and it is therefore thought that they are less likely to want a leadership position. Women therefore have to fight more for the positions they want. Having regular catch-ups with your manager can help here. Women need to make it clear how they want their career to progress from the get-go and not let these assumptions stop them from getting to where they want to be.

Creating a support network can be more of a challenge for women. Because men have dominated for so long, they have a stronger support network to draw upon. Many 'men only' clubs still exist. But finding a common cause with other women can be very powerful. It's not in many management textbooks, I shouldn't think, but the Grunwick Strike is a really good example. In 1976, women were not powerful at work in the UK, and uneducated South Asian women in particular were among the least powerful employees, doing the least skilled factory jobs. But six women walking out of their workplace led to one of the most important industrial actions of that decade. Though ultimately their fight was unsuccessful, it transformed the trade unions from white, male organizations to more inclusive bodies that maintained the rights of women and POC (people of color) – a really huge change. I am a member of a 'women in tax' network. It has become a great support network of women helping other women in their careers. Look for networks that you can get involved in or even better, start one yourself! It could have a really positive impact on your career and your confidence.

When you're working with other women, you can start addressing some of the specific roadblocks to women's leadership. You can address other women's imposter syndrome and help them overcome perfectionism and lack of confidence; you can help them ask for money, whether that's a hike in salary, or the money to start their own business or project. If you become a member of the C-suite, you'll be a role model for other women, and you can help ensure your organization's management is female-friendly. You can encourage each other; women working with other women often feel more confident than women in a mainly male environment. So, build a 'sisterhood', supporting and empowering other women, and you'll find it will benefit you too.

Stumbling blocks for women	How to overcome them
Men get more opportunities than women	Keep asking for opportunities you want
Women lack in confidence more than men	Use confident body language. Don't second guess yourself. Take feedback on the chin
Taking time out from their career to have/raise a family	Build up your network again after taking a career break and make it clear you're committed to moving forward
Women find it harder to make themselves heard	Speak up in meetings
The workplace doesn't expect women to want leadership roles	Have regular catch ups with your manager and let them know you want progression
Men have a stronger support network	Join female only networks or create one yourself! Help other women, support each other

Chapter Three
LEARN THE SECRETS OF THE
MOST SUCCESSFUL WOMEN

R eal leadership comes from within. It's born when you have something you really want to achieve. Sometimes you'll feel it like a fire burning inside. It's determination, perseverance, grit, vision.

But it's also something you learn. You need to understand how to get things rolling, how to motivate other people, and the technical and soft skills you need.

Some leaders are born leaders. Others are made. Both have to learn on their way.

So, in this chapter, I want to look at successful women and what made them successful.

Successful leadership traits in other women

Determination
Beth E. Mooney, CEO of Keycorp and first CEO of a top American bank, had real determination. She was working as a bank secretary when she

decided she wanted a place on a bank management training scheme. She ended up refusing to leave the scheme manager's office till she had persuaded him to give her a place. That's determination.

Openness

Claire Watts, CEO of retail company QVC, has regular 'open door' slots for anyone in the business to come talk to her about whatever they like. Young interns can keep her up to date with youth fashion or social media, or someone with a new product idea can take it straight to the top, but she may also end up talking about people's families or football teams.

Her open door keeps her up with the trends, but it also makes employees feel that they're valued, not just as workers but as people.

Assertiveness

Assertiveness means being able to state your opinion decisively, and to take control of your own career, for instance by negotiating on your own behalf. Women often don't ask for a raise – that's one reason that after ten or twenty years of their careers they may be earning significantly less than men at their level. Yes, it's a risk. It's scary, for many women. You run the risk of refusal, and when you've been socialized to believe that your job is pleasing other people, that can really hurt. But you need to learn.

Sonia Sotomayor, associate justice of the US Supreme Court, said in an interview with Der Spiegel: "There's nothing wrong with being a little bit quieter than me or more timid than me, but if you're doing it all of the time and not waiting for the moments where you need to be more assertive and take greater control, then you won't be successful."

Curiosity

Maria Moraes Robinson is CEO of business consultancy Holonomics. She says: "Never be afraid to embrace your curiosity." Finding out about things is a key skill and increases your ability to embrace a variety of roles and subjects. Curiosity is one of the top skills that female leaders exhibit – asking questions, probing, asking "What if?", looking outside the usual places to find knowledge. Never stop asking questions or being curious about other people's lives and interests. Never stop learning!

Visibility

Women in corporate life sometimes retreat into the background, doing important jobs but never claiming the limelight. Many women have been socialized that way: we are taught not to make too much noise, not to blow your own trumpet, not to be 'forward.' But Former US Attorney General Loretta Lynch says: "I always tell young women, make yourself seen, and make yourself heard – this is your idea, this is your thought. Own it, express it, be the voice that people hear."

You may have other superpowers. You may be a great problem-solver, a great story-teller, a motivator, or a nurturing leader. Whatever your superpowers are, find them, and use them. Create your own personal profile or 'brand.'

Power, influence, profile and other useful things to think about

It can be helpful to understand the difference between power and influence – and which you intend to exercise. Influence is indirect; you have to exercise it through other people. Power is something different; you can exercise it directly. Power, according to Nancy Pelosi, is "the ability to make change." Influence can help, but power actually gets it done.

Women often have issues with power. They don't like 'power over' others. They don't seek it, and they're not comfortable with it. But if you rephrase it as 'power to achieve things,' you've transformed your relationship with power. Power becomes a tool you can use to achieve justice, to make other people's lives better, or to advance knowledge. That's why it's worth seeking power – the power to transform yourself and other women in your business.

You need to create a 'moving train,' to make yourself look as if you are moving forward and achieving things. Successful women build themselves a profile as a woman who is going places; if you this, you will find other people want to support you, or to come along on the ride.

Successful women use mentors as supporters. While some firms have mentoring schemes, you could also look for your own mentors outside the organization, perhaps in your professional body. But don't ask point blank: "Will you be my mentor?" That's way too formal, unless it's in a formally based scheme. Instead, just put the conditions in place where someone might take an interest in your career. Send an email to keep in touch, send an article you found interesting, or put them in touch with someone who can help them. Maintain the relationship. Then later on, you might just say you are thinking through a couple of important issues and ask if they would mind you using them as a sounding board.

Make sure other people in your life support you, particularly men – fathers, brothers, a male partner, peers and mentors. That's important, because you may sometimes need to see things from a male perspective. Of course, the support of women in your family is equally important. Let them understand what drives you, and why you care so much about it.

(By the way, if you encounter bad behavior from men in your workplace, don't accept it; challenge it. If a man speaks through you, take it on. If you offer an idea in a meeting and then a man restates your idea and claims the credit, challenge him).

We touched on this in an earlier chapter but successful women free themselves up by delegating - delegating is not lazy. If you read classical economic theory, you'll come across the idea of specialization; for instance, the theory says, countries should specialize in things they're good at, and buy in other things from abroad. That way, the most efficient country always gets to make the relevant goods. Use the right specialized talents in the right place. And don't think delegating is "because you can't do it all" (although it's true, you can't); delegation is about enabling your entire team to accomplish more, by making sure everyone is doing the things they're best able to do.

If you want to be successful, you'll need to prioritize ruthlessly. Women often say "yes" to far too many responsibilities and tasks. Do the things which are really important. Don't get distracted into activities which are not important for your organization and not important for your personal or career development.

A trap some women fall into is creating their own glass ceilings by staying in their comfort zones. Learn to seek fear and discomfort – to start with, in quite small quantities – successful women learn new skills, experience new environments, and stretch themselves. For instance, you may not have applied for promotions in the past because you feared rejection. You need to get happy with the word 'no.' Just consider it means "not this time, but maybe later," and you may be able to handle it more easily.

If you want to be successful, hire people who are smarter than you. That might mean technically smart (IT people, engineers, finance wizards, graphic artists, marketing consultants) or it might mean problem-solving and practical 'street smart,' or it might just mean having people on your team who you know will always get to the solution a microsecond before you do. Great equestrians know they will always get the gold medals when they ride a horse with character, a horse with a mind of its own. The same goes for managers and teams: don't hire 'safe' people, hire people who will make your job an enjoyable challenge.

Taking your own time

One thing that's common to many high-achieving women is that they get up early. They can then have a free hour in the morning to jog, meditate, or simply relax without any pressure (there's also scientific evidence that 'morning people' get higher grades as students, and are likely to be more optimistic and proactive).

Women often don't take time for themselves; there's always someone else wanting them to do something, whether that's a partner, child, customer, or manager. Make sure you have your own time for exercise and for relaxation; it makes a big difference. Make sure, if you get up early, that you don't burn the candle at both ends; you'll need your sleep. Don't sacrifice sleep in order to get more done, because you'll end up undermining your ability to get much done at all! My morning routine consists of either going to the gym at 6am or exercising at home and doing some yoga and meditation before work. I really feel the benefits of this.

And don't feel guilty about taking the time. As if life weren't tough enough, the media love to tell us how we should feel guilty if we can't be a supermodel, devoted mom, wonderful wife, Fortune 500 CEO, charity volunteer, *and* play piano to professional level at the same time. Sometimes you need to say "no." "No, I can't come to every single football game you play." "No, we can't have a barbecue; I need some time to myself this weekend." "No, I can't replace our CFO at short notice for that trip to San Diego; it's my grandmother's 100th birthday." You know what's important to you; keep that in mind and don't let other people run your to-do list.

You don't need to be performing at 100% all the time. Sometimes you will want to slow down a little and think, sometimes you can coast, sometimes you need to catch your breath. If you are trying to be 100% every second, you're behaving like the guy who can't help revving up his Ferrari at the traffic lights. Work has a natural rhythm. Watch a good craftsperson and you'll see how they instinctively know when to go in heavy, and when to use a more delicate touch. Let that natural rhythm get started, and you'll often be able to go with the flow.

You don't have to do everything. You don't have to do it all perfectly. Knowing your priorities and running your life the way *you* need to is absolutely key to success, whether you're running a world-class IT company, playing double bass in a jazz band, or writing the Great American Novel, or just trying to keep your small business making a profit.

Another aspect of time is knowing when to move on. Many women stay in 'number two' jobs long after they should have taken over their own division or company. It's comfortable. Or they long to get international experience, but since their current company doesn't have an overseas business, they give up on the dream. Remember that in many companies or careers, there's an age structure to careers: it's noticeable when someone becomes the youngest-ever divisional head in a company, but on the downside, you may end up considered a bit on the old side for taking on your first operational role. So, you want to give that some thought when you're making your plans.

Look at your career and where you want it to go. See where you are on that journey; it's like reading a map. Is taking this path going to get you where you need to be as a great leader?

Passion

One final factor that links successful women is that they believe in themselves because they have a passion. Look at some of the young women who have made their mark over the past decade. Greta Thunberg owes her influence to her real passion for the environment. Malala Yousafzai cares deeply about educating girls and giving them life choices. Simone Biles is not only an amazing gymnast but also speaks openly about mental health issues and ADHD.

You have a passion somewhere. Maybe it's a passion for information architecture and cybersecurity. Maybe it's a passion for ice cream. Maybe it's a desire for justice. Believing in that passion is the first step to believing in yourself.

Once you've found your passion, you can find your superpower. And when you know that superpower, you can rock your superpower, whether it's "there is no legal precedent of which she's unaware," "the hottest coder in open source," or "she's so persuasive she could get the Grinch to enjoy Christmas."

Examples of successful women

Angela Merkel

Chancellor of Germany for sixteen years, and considered de facto leader of the European Union, Angela Merkel didn't start off as a politician. She was a research scientist with a doctorate in quantum chemistry. It was only after the fall of the Berlin Wall that she became involved with politics. She was a real outsider, an 'Ossi' (East German) in the new reunified Germany, with no political background, and female in what is still a very male-dominated society.

Merkel was never afraid to take an uncompromising and unpopular position. For instance, in 2015, she announced that Germany would take migrants fleeing Syria even if they had come through other EU countries, though the law said they should apply for asylum in the first country they reached. She was always prepared to speak out if she had to.

But she was also a leader who worked hard to support the European Union and to strengthen cooperation between EU nations, for instance leading much of the work on a post-Covid reconstruction package. She made a practice of looking for cooperation rather than confrontation, and gave people confidence with her watchword: "Wir schaffen das" – "We can do it."

Joey Wat, CEO, Yum China

If you want a real 'rags to riches' story, Joey Wat is exactly that, progressing from child factory worker making plastic flowers to chief executive of a huge company. And she achieved all that in a society that still sees women as, in many ways second-class citizens.

Joey took a risk early in her career. She was a management consultant, then moved into the role of managing director at the struggling Savers health and beauty chain. It could have gone badly wrong. She managed to save the business, getting it into profit, and saving thousands of jobs. She calls it a "scary" learning experience, but an important one.

When Covid forced Yum China to close its stores to the public, she tried to find a way to keep her employees in work. Yum China provided free meals to essential workers, hospitals and community centers, and that enabled her to keep a number of the restaurants open. She also started up a number of 'angel' restaurants which supported workers with disabilities.

Clearly, her early experience has given her the ability to empathize with ordinary employees. And she points out that in any career, "Sometimes the right thing is not the easy path."

Julie Sweet, CEO, Accenture

Julie Sweet was number nine on Fortune's 2019 list of Most Powerful Women, but she's humble enough to share her own learning blog. She talks about what she's learning, and how. Her commitment to continued self-improvement is an inspiration; she leads by example.

Throughout her career, she has decided what her new job should be by asking herself "What is the role where I can make the biggest impact?" There's no doubt that the role she's now in gives her a huge ability to influence corporate cultures across the world.

Julie Hanna, Executive Chair, Kiva

Kiva is an international non-profit which brings funding to unbanked people around the world. Whether it's fertilizers for a women-run farm in Kenya or new sewing machines for a small business in Pakistan, Kiva works with microcredit partners to match crowdfunded deposits with small businesses needing loans.

Julie Hanna has been at the head of numerous Silicon Valley companies including Healtheon, onebox.com and Scalix. She's also been a key early-stage investor in successful firms like Lyft. But she's particularly proud of her work at Kiva, empowering individuals to achieve their potential.

She's a real outsider – a Coptic Christian, war refugee, and immigrant American – and she's used her empathy to become a thought-leader in the fields of purpose-driven profit, non-profits, and the use of technology to empower people and create a fairer world.

STEPS TO GREAT LEADERSHIP

Step One
KNOW THE DIFFERENCE BETWEEN MANAGEMENT AND LEADERSHIP

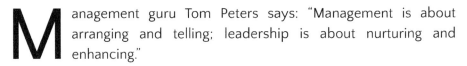

Management guru Tom Peters says: "Management is about arranging and telling; leadership is about nurturing and enhancing."

Jack Welch, former GE Chairman and CEO said: "Before you are a leader, success is all about growing yourself. When you become a leader, success is all about growing others."

There's a big, big difference between being a leader and being a manager.

If you ask yourself the following questions, you'll soon find out which of the two you are right now:

- Do you inspire your team?
- Do all your team feel they can speak to you about anything that's on their mind?
- Does everyone you're responsible for know what's going on and how they fit in?
- Do you delegate authority?

- Do you encourage team members and act as a part of the team?
- When there's a mess, do you resist the temptation to look for a scapegoat?

If you answered 'no' more often than 'yes,' you're probably a manager. If you answered 'yes,' you're on the way to becoming a leader.

There's another question that often finds out the 'bosses' too: How many of your staff have quit in the last year? A study by GoodHire showed that 82% of professionals they surveyed would consider quitting their job if they had a bad boss. In many sectors, like hospitality, turnover is very high, but good leadership can keep people with the business and cut down the cost of hiring and training new staff, as well as maintaining morale.

So, let's sum up a few of the differences between managers and leaders. Start thinking about how you can adopt qualities of a leader as you progress in your role.

Manager v leader

Managers command. Leaders influence

Some bosses are not much better than a parent who tells children to do something "because I said so." It may get the job done, but it won't do more.

Instead, a leader will talk about the vision, how the thing they're asking for fits in, and why they're asking this particular team member to do it. If there is an objection, they'll listen – perhaps the team member doesn't actually have the technical skills to deliver the work package, or it's the first time they've worked at this level and they lack confidence.

Leaders also know that relationships work both ways, so they actively seek their team members' buy-in. For a leader, it's not enough to get a grudging "okay"; they want to know that team members fully understand the overall vision and can commit to it. They want their team to share their vision, not just accept it.

Sometimes you can even leave the decisions on who does what up to your team – *if* you've empowered your team and they're ready for it.

Managers focus on the process. Leaders focus on the outcome

Bosses are great ones for job manuals, protocols, and the status quo. They want things done 'the right way.' Leaders are less worried about the process; they will innovate and develop new ways of working, while keeping the long-term goal in mind. The boss says: "Take the subway to Broadway Junction"; the leader says: "Be at Broadway Junction by two" and leaves it up to the team member to decide whether they'll walk, take the subway, taxi, bike, or parachute in from a plane (though that would probably be excessive, particularly if the budget is tight).

Managers explain. Leaders inspire, support, and guide

Two different carpentry firms worked on my house at different times. Both the carpenters had apprentices. Mr A just explained the task to be done, gave the girl her tools, and went to work on something else. Mr B, on the other hand, cut one of the two mortises for the door himself, explaining what he was doing as he did it, and then asked his young lad to cut the second one. He stayed there, ready to give support, warn when things weren't going quite right, and give tips on how to straighten the cut properly and how to tell when it was deep enough.

Both those apprentices succeeded in their careers and are now master carpenters, but both of them are now working for Mr B! Meanwhile, Mr A is finding it difficult to hire new help.

"If your actions inspire others to dream more, learn more, do more and become more, you are a leader." – President John Quincy Adams.

Managers discipline and blame. Leaders mentor and support

A reward and punishment system is easy to install, but it doesn't always get the best out of team members. Worse, it can lead to them being unwilling to innovate or take risks, so you will get a predictable but mediocre result.

Leaders, instead, prefer to mentor their teams, helping employees acquire new skills and build confidence. A leader will develop the team's skills in order to meet future challenges successfully, rather than simply focusing on performing the task in hand. Leaders will not just train team members in particular skills but will help them plan their own learning and development.

If you have a team with different levels of experience, try to find mentors for the less experienced. In my company, we always assign a buddy to the newest members of the team, someone with more experience who can guide and help them.

Managers delegate individual tasks. Leaders delegate authority

Bosses often delegate tasks or action points, but specify them very tightly and are likely to dictate how the tasks are done. They are concerned that their team members 'get it right.' A leader, on the other hand, delegates the authority for carrying out a particular part of the plan. They enable team members to understand the overall vision, and then expect them to simply 'do the right thing.' It's the difference between having a tick list and having a common goal.

Managers focus on tasks. Leaders focus on the team

Bosses tend to be task-focused. They have a list of things to get done, or a process to administer. That's why they delegate tasks, small packages of work. Leaders, on the other hand, will get tasks done, but they go beyond looking at today's to-do list; they think about getting their team ready for *future* challenges. Whether they're natural 'people persons' or not, they know that they have to think about people and the team they're building, not just about action points.

Managers have subordinates. Leaders have co-workers

The whole idea of a 'boss' is hierarchical. They are told what to do by their boss, then they tell their subordinates what to do, and those subordinates might in turn tell other people what to do. A leader, on the other hand, sees all members of the team as individuals who can contribute to the team goal. They also see them as personalities, rather than just cogs in a machine, so they care about their team members' personal and career development.

A boss will apply the same levers to get things done no matter who he or she is talking to. A leader knows that some team members need coaxing and supporting, while others can just be let loose – and are in fact happier going solo to get their part of the project done.

In fact, bosses tend to see their whole job in terms of the organizational hierarchy. They will follow official channels to achieve their objectives and stay within their own reporting chain. Leaders, on the other hand, will break down 'silos' within the organization and will do what is needed, whether that's going right to the top to plead the case for a particular project, or talking to front line managers in another department to find out what's blocking a development. They may even decide the organization itself needs changing.

"To lead people, walk beside them. As for the best leaders, the people do not notice their existence... When the best leader's work is done, the people say, 'We did it ourselves!'" – Lao Tzu, philosopher.

Managers don't take risks. Leaders can take big risks

Most bosses are not risk takers. They do the safe thing. They achieve what they're asked to, and they don't rock the boat.

Leaders will take risks if they need to. Sometimes, they will take big risks, like Joey Wat taking on the 'mission not quite impossible' of rescuing a failing business.

Managers give directions. Leaders ask questions

"Work out the profit margin on this" becomes "Just how profitable could this product be?"

"I need it by Monday" becomes "How quickly could you get this done?"

"We'd better get this sorted" becomes "How could we fix this?"

Managers tell you what. Leaders show you how

"This is the way we do budgets here." "Okay, let me take you through this, we do a few things differently – have you used zero-based budgeting before? Okay, basically how it works is... and then from there, you can fill in this number here."

When I mentioned the two carpenters, you can see how the second one actually showed how to cut a mortice before giving his apprentice the chance to do it with support. As President Theodore Roosevelt once said, "People ask the difference between a leader and a boss. The leader leads, and the boss drives."

Managers use reason. Leaders understand emotion

Managers usually stay aloof; they are scientific, rational, and practical. Leaders, on the other hand, are fully aware of the emotional aspects of their job, so they will try to inspire and support their staff emotionally as well as practically. They will create excitement and commitment.

A boss will say: "We need to get from here to Winterton." A leader might say: "Winterton's a marvellous place, and there will be a cream tea laid on for us! Let's get there as fast as we can!"

(Don't fake it, though. There's nothing worse than the corporate mission fake. We've all met one).

Managers see detail. Leaders see the big picture

Managers usually manage their team as a glorified tick box, adding together small action points to achieve their objectives. A + B + C = Job Done. Leaders, on the other hand, see the big picture, so they understand how their teams' output fits in the enterprise as a whole. For instance, a manager will keep a manufacturing process turning out product even if sales have headed downwards and the inventory is building up. A leader will see the build-up of inventory, and ask questions about whether that's deliberate, whether they should think about cutting production, and whether they'll need to make it more efficient to compete at lower prices.

Once you see the big picture it's easy to show it to your team. It's so simple.

Managers react to change. Leaders create it

Think about two teams of lumberjacks. A boss will find out how to cut down trees more quickly and efficiently. A leader will think about why the trees are being cut: Is it to build a road or a city, to build houses, for cooking fuel? A leader might, in the end, come up with an idea for stoves that use less fuel, or decide that clearcutting (cutting every tree in a section of forest) can be replaced by cutting only one in every ten trees, leaving the rest of the forest to regenerate.

All of these small differences add up to one big difference.

Bosses manage things adequately in the short term. In fact, if you are a good manager rather than a 'bad boss,' there's definitely a place for you in any organization. But it won't be right at the top. It won't be at the cutting edge.

Leaders manage for the long term, empowering and developing employees, innovating, and working towards a long-term vision. They lay the groundwork for the future and create the next generation of leaders.

If you own your own business, though, you'll need to be *both* a manager *and* a leader to get the best out of it. Even if you're an independent freelancer, you might exercise leadership in your professional area; for instance, as a change consultant you might take on the task of being a figurehead for the profession, giving talks, joining companies as an adviser, being 'Ms Change.'

Are leaders born or made?

Some leadership qualities are innate. Some people seem born brave – never afraid to take a risk or fight for what's right. Some people have natural charisma. Others, like the Dalai Lama, have huge compassion. Some people are good collaborators by nature.

But one quality doesn't make a leader. You could be incredibly courageous but completely unable to inspire others. You could have great charisma, but your chances could be blown when people realize you have no integrity. You could be compassionate but unable to inspire others. Being a leader involves putting all these different qualities together. The Dalai Lama became a leader the day he left Tibet for India and decided to fight the Tibetan people's cause internationally.

Training and experience can help you become a great leader. Seek out experiences that will test you, like difficult projects, or speaking assignments. You can train in interpersonal skills such as active listening or negotiation, just as you can train in technical skills like finance, JavaScript, or marketing.

You'll also need to acquire the ability to withstand stress, to delegate, and to have the patience not to check up on team members you've delegated to every five minutes, 'just in case.' And you'll need plenty of introspection, thinking about your management style and how you can improve it.

So don't say: "I'm not a leader" just because you weren't a sports captain at school, or because you're not gregarious (you're definitely not the first person to ask "Do I really have to go to that networking event?"). The question is really whether you want to be a great leader and whether you're prepared to do what it takes to become one.

In the next chapter, we are going to talk in more detail about the steps you can take to prepare for leadership right away.

Step Two
USE POWERFUL FEMALE TRAITS TO YOUR ADVANTAGE

Are there common traits that make women successful?

Thereis still aren't enough female leaders in the world. Women don't even make up 10% of CEOs at Fortune 500 companies, though 2021 saw them hit an all-time record of forty-one CEOs, including two black women, Roz Brewer at Walgreens and Thasunda Brown Duckett at TIAA, and including Beth Ford, the first openly gay female CEO of a Fortune 500 company. In politics, women still make up a minority of leaders at top levels, though the US now has a female VP, France has a female prime minister, and in the small Eastern European state of Moldova, both the president and the prime minister are women.

Most of these women could tell you they've had to prove themselves on multiple occasions. They likely feel they have to work harder than their male peers, and in some cases, they will have had to try extremely hard to gain respect from male co-workers. So, the first of the great common traits they have is strength. They're strong enough to deal with stereotypes, to stand up for what they believe in, to make an impact, and to believe in themselves. They've also had to demonstrate real perseverance to get where they are. Jobs don't fall into their laps. Sometimes, they're discouraged from 'male' disciplines such as the sciences or finance, and they've had to push hard to be accepted. They've needed to show adaptability, perhaps managing to bring up a young family and be a corporate leader at the same time. They may have needed to move company to find an environment that would let them develop their careers. And often, they have had to know how to ask for what they want in terms of career development or opportunities, because they've been overlooked time and again for promotions or high-profile projects, and they've also had to learn how to politely ignore mansplaining and other bad advice.

Men don't usually get challenged so directly, but if you're female, plenty of people who have no experience or expertise in your area will be willing to give you their opinions. Molly Scott-Cato, Green MEP, was taunted in the European Parliament for knowing nothing about economics. She responded, more politely than most people would have done, that she's actually a professor of economics and has published widely on the subject!

Finally, the next generation of women leaders are no longer flying solo, as their mothers and grandmothers had to do. They see other women at all levels in their organizations. And they now have the chance to create female-empowered workplaces. During Covid, for instance, many women found themselves working from home, but with schools closed, that also meant having small kids in the 'office'; unsurprisingly, they're now burned out. Paying attention to specific female needs such as support for childcare issues and help for women with low self-confidence can make a huge difference.

Women can make great leaders for many reasons. Of course, we shouldn't stereotype female leaders – some women are very task-orientated, and can't multi-task for toffee – but we can identify some broad strengths. Here are a few.

Women tend to value work-life balance and emotions

Many women have their own children to look after – a role which is still often unequally shared between the partners. They understand the needs for work-life balance of others in their teams and offer flexibility.

Women are also brought up to care about personal emotions in a way that many men aren't. They care about their team's wellbeing where a male leader might only care about the performance figures. That's shown in the fact that women volunteer for mentorship and training roles in much greater proportions than men.

Women are inclusive

Some work environments become dominated by a narrow clique of people all from the same background. One of my friends was the only woman in a finance firm. Later, she found out she was also the only person in management who hadn't been in the army, and the only one who hadn't been to a private school.

Men very often recruit people like themselves, sometimes without realizing it. Women tend to be more inclusive, not just in recruitment but in reaching out to other people and other departments. Women tend to talk more in the 'we' because they realize the power of the team is diversity and the best teams have different kinds of skills and thought leadership. If we were all the same, companies wouldn't evolve.

Women have intuition

Of course, both men and women have intuition but there may actually be science behind what we call 'women's intuition.' Women show great ability to draw insight from what seems intangible, is, in fact, just heightened sensory ability because we use our senses to pick up on things others may miss. Research on non-verbal communication has shown that women are better at reading facial expressions in general, so can pick up more subtle emotional messages.

It has long been ignored in the workplace but is a necessary skill for success.

Women show empathy

Every person brings their head and their heart to their work and leaders need to see that their work is deeply human. But it can often be overlooked. Many of the challenges leaders face elicit an intellectual or emotional response.

Effective leaders embody traits such as empathy and emotion because people want to feel heard and understood and these traits are needed to connect on a human level by engaging the heart and employing storytelling. Debra Bednar-Clark, an executive coach and Founder and CEO of DB&co states, "as a leader, you have to have empathy and curiosity to understand who someone is at their core: their goals, fears, aspirations, passions, insecurities—all of it. Then you can help them double down on their strengths and overcome their barriers, so they can make an impact that is authentic to them and of value to the business."

One of the reasons New Zealand's Prime Minister Jacinda Ardern has impressed so many people is that she displays clear empathy with others. For instance, after a mosque shooting in Christchurch, she wore a hijab to show respect for local Muslims and reached out to hug one woman who had lost a relative. She also pledged financial assistance to bereaved families. Empathy isn't just about hugs; it's also about understanding how you can help others practically.

Empathy can help the less confident members of a team to blossom. It can help you understand your customers better. And a lot of leaders appreciate empathy from their teams, too, as leading isn't always an easy job.

Men can show empathy too, but unlike women, they're often socialised not to do so, or shown as weak or powerless when they do.

Women are good at multitasking

Not all women are good at multitasking, of course! But most women, because they've had to combine child-raising with a career, or been tasked to look after smaller siblings while doing their homework, know what having to multitask means. They get used to it.

Leaders need to multitask.

If you remember 'Q' in the James Bond films, he never gets any further up the hierarchy – he's a nerd inventor playing in his laboratory. He's not a leader; he can only do one thing. Mind you, he does it well – without his help, Bond wouldn't get very far; he'd probably have ended up in the piranha pool already (there's room for specialists as well as leaders in the world – but make sure you know which you'd rather be).

You probably have people like that on your team. But to manage a project, for instance, you'll need to be thinking about customers, team members, other stakeholders, the task, checking up on progress, ensuring your objectives are still in line with the overall vision for the project, and quite likely delivering your own work packages and action points too. You may also need to help a staff member who is struggling with a promotion, and think about appropriate training for one of your team who could take on more responsibility.

Women can also 'wear many hats.' They may balance looking after elderly parents or children with a career as well as finding time to exercise and get involved with local activities. So, they can switch between managerial, mentoring, and counseling roles easily.

Women defy the odds
This, unlike the categories above, really does apply to all women. They started with a disadvantage in corporate life and the closer they get to the top, the more they're in the minority.

There are also a few things women leaders could teach men:

If you've nothing to say, don't say it
Stats show that fewer women than men ask questions after presentations, or volunteer to speak at events. But that doesn't mean that they don't have any questions, or that they have nothing to say. Rather, it means that men tend to pursue those opportunities just so that they will get noticed. Men

often 'lean in' – assert themselves, brag, take credit – and traditionally, it's worked for them. Increasingly, though, their bluff is being called.

Inspire, don't command

Female leaders often lead through example and inspiration. They also help transform their team and its members by giving the team a meaning and a purpose, a buy-in to the vision behind the project. Men often adopt an approach which is about analyzing, handing out roles, and tasking team members with delivery dates, without trying to win 'hearts and minds.' A bit more inspiration from some male leaders wouldn't go amiss.

Act as a talent agent and help others up

The 'slippery slope' or 'greasy pole' most men try to climb doesn't have room for other people on it. Women in management tend to be much less obsessed with reaching the top on their own, and more interested in mentoring, and in developing and promoting their team members. Male leaders who try to nurture other members of their networks may find that behaviour works better than traditional office politics.

Be more self-aware

Many men are overconfident. They're *sure* they have what it takes. Women are often more realistic about their own limitations. That can work against women, of course, in that they don't put themselves forwards for promotion because they don't feel confident. But it can also work for them, because when you're realistic about your limitations, that's a first step to getting training, experience or expertise that can help you address and overcome them.

Demonstrate emotional intelligence!

On the whole, most women have a bit more 'EQ' than most men. We're brought up that way. So, if you've got it, use it: anticipate how members of your team will feel about things, and have a plan to deal with that.

Show resilience

Most women who have reached the top will tell you they've met numerous setbacks on the way. You can't afford to give up. Some men will push you hard, hoping you will take the easy option. Don't. Fortunately, any woman who has had to deal with managing younger siblings, or children, or getting accepted in STEM subjects has already learned that resilience.

Keep their ego in check

Yes, women have egos too, but we're not generally brought up to blow our own trumpets the way men do. While you need to learn to claim your successes, don't make the mistake of letting your ego run wild. Just stay grounded and realistic and you'll be able to run rings round the guys (and some women) with big egos who will throw a huge sulk about not having a corner office but won't actually achieve the results to go with it!

Communication skills that put women at an advantage

One of the big differences between men and women is the way they tend to communicate. It's a stark cultural difference. Things may be changing with the latest generation, but most men and women have been raised in similar gender-based ways, which have affected the ways they tend to express themselves and also how they understand others.

Poor communication can lead to poor performance. Productivity can suffer, and goals may be missed. A 2016 study by David Grossman, 'The Cost of Poor Communications,' found that larger companies lost an average $62.4m a year just through not communicating well enough internally. Ordering the wrong component, leaving ambiguous instructions that have to be checked, and similar inadequate communications can all cost real money.

But equally, poor communication can stifle innovation, demotivate employees, and prevent staff understanding the business vision and mission.

Differences between men and women

Men tend to like 'banter' – trash talking, competitive boasting, and so on. Women very often regard it as somewhat hostile; when women are together, they don't usually talk in this way (however, women in a male-dominated environment often learn to talk like the men).

In meetings, men will frequently interrupt each other. They will even *more* frequently interrupt women. Women in meetings will usually let everyone have their say.

Showing sensitivity and concern for others, and bringing quieter participants into the conversation, are typical feminine traits. But men (and some women) will see anyone displaying such traits as a 'supporter' rather than a leader.

Men often dislike having to show ignorance or weakness. They won't usually ask for feedback, whereas women often will. And men often will be silent rather than asking a question that shows they don't understand a particular topic. Women are more likely to ask for an explanation or definition, but this risks men seeing it as incompetence or lack of expertise, rather than as an attempt to clarify or ensure everyone is properly informed.

Men also tend to like factual topics and information. A masculine work culture generally won't spend much time discussing whether everyone's objectives are aligned, or how people feel about a particular course of action. Women often prefer to spend time building relationships and generating rapport first. That's also a feature of some other cultures; for instance, in Japan, building a relationship with a customer or supplier always comes before discussing business.

Women tend to apologize more often. That can be seen as an admission of weakness. You'll often hear a woman at a meeting say, "I'm sorry, I don't agree." Many women will also take great care not to come across as 'pushy' or aggressive. They'll start a contribution by saying "I'm not an expert, but..." The difficulty here is that many male-orientated cultures will interpret this kind of communication as showing the woman is unambitious, disengaged, or even incompetent, whereas for women, such tags are just ways of lubricating a discussion.

Women also tend to acknowledge points that other people have made much more often than most men do. They are more likely to try to bring other people into the conversation, rather than trying to boost themselves. These are behaviors most of us learned from mothers and grandmothers, even before we went to school.

Women may tend to seek approval rather than trying to dominate. There aren't a lot of 'alpha females.'

Sometimes, they'll try to gain approval by disclaiming their own competence, since men in particular often see competence in a woman as an unlikeable trait (however, when your mom knew how to do everything, like tie your shoes or help you with your math homework, you loved her, right? Society is very screwed up on this particular matter).

Women will often collaborate rather than competing. That's an advantage in many modern enterprises where collaboration is important. For instance, many craft brewers collaborate extensively with other micro-breweries, hold beer festivals, and run 'tap takeovers' with bars, all supporting each other in order to grow customer demand and create a market for premium beers. Technology companies also collaborate, swapping programming interfaces so they can use each other's programs and create joint projects.

There are some neurological differences between men and women. For instance, men tend to release testosterone, women oxytocin. Oxytocin produces a feeling of mutual trust. But under high stress, oxytocin stops and the testosterone wins out. So when women experience high stress levels, whilst the oxytocin seems to stop, testosterone and adrenalin continue to be released so the 'male' behaviors tend to prevail when stress is above a certain level. Another explanation for different responses to stress are that men have a 'fight or flight' response while women are educated to have a 'tend or befriend' response – such as trying to talk their way out of a tricky situation. That can mean collaboration breaks down when the going gets tough.

Something women can do that men often won't is to ask for help. That doesn't mean doing a Lady Penelope Pitstop and shouting "Help!" every time something goes wrong, but when you're coming way out of your comfort zone, it means explaining that you are doing something difficult and to ask for support. Men who fail often do so because they wouldn't ask for help or wouldn't solicit feedback.

Good communication traits that come easily to women

Now that we have looked at the differences between the way men and women communicate, we're going to discuss what good communication looks like. Most of what I am going to talk about comes easily to women but if you notice any that may be a struggle to you, that nay be a sign that you need more practice or training in this area.

Learning to communicate better is good for every leader, not just women. For instance, you should learn to adapt your style depending on who you're talking to. You should also learn how to listen actively: take notes, ask questions to clarify ("You mean financially?") or explore ("And how did customers feel about the product?"). Don't let yourself be distracted; give the person you're listening to your full attention, even if it's just for a couple of minutes.

Open-ended questions are a great way to get team members to talk and women are great at this. All journalists learn to ask the key questions: "who, what, why, where, how?" You'll also want to use phrases like, "Tell me more," or, "Can you define that?"

Transparency is very important in building trust. Make sure all your people know what's happening, all the time. Be open about your goals, challenges, and how your team is doing. Make sure everyone understands their role and how their work fits into the team and company. Don't rely on a game of broken telephone to deliver the message – it will get twisted in the process.

(In the First World War, apparently a captain at the front sent back a message: "Send us reinforcements, we are going to advance." By the time it had passed through two field telephones and a couple of messengers, the message had become "Send us three and fourpence, we are going to a dance").

Pay attention to body language. This is something women, particularly in Asian cultures, may find difficult because the body language that leaders use runs counter to what they were brought up to do. For instance, many women avoid eye contact with men, but in a work context, that can make you look shifty, furtive and untrustworthy. Many women try to make themselves small and not take up too much space; again, our view of 'leadership' is someone standing tall.

Ask for feedback and give it. Remember that if you ask for feedback, you need to acknowledge it and, if possible, act on it. Otherwise, people won't see why you're asking for feedback if you don't appear to value it. When you give feedback, remember 'the sandwich' – praise, constructive criticism, praise. That way, you can advise a member of staff on how to improve, while leaving them feeling appreciated and successful.

So, on your way to great leadership, you're going to need to start building new skills. Pay attention to the way you communicate at work and change things that aren't working for you. Build new skills through training schemes, reading, and networking events, and through experiences which will stretch you. Come out of your comfort zone and reach for the stars.

GOOD COMMUNICATION SKILLS

- Adapt your style depending on who you're talking to
- Practice active listening
- Ask questions to clarify
- Ask lots of open-ended questions
- Don't get distracted

- Be transparent
- Use appropriate body language
- Ask for and give feedback
- Get involved in experiences that will stretch you

Step Three
OVERCOME IMPOSTER SYNDROME AND SELF-DOUBT

Let's start this chapter by asking: Who might have said these things?

1. "I have spent my years since Princeton, while at law school and in my various professional jobs, not feeling completely a part of the worlds I inhabit. I am always looking over my shoulder, wondering if I measure up."

2. "Each time I write a book, every time I face that yellow pad, the challenge is so great. I have written eleven books, but each time I think, 'Uh oh, they're going to find out now. I've run a game on everybody and they're going to find me out.'"

3. "Now when I receive recognition for my acting, I feel incredibly uncomfortable. I tend to turn in on myself. I feel like an imposter."

Number one: Sonia Sotomayor, the first Hispanic lawyer to serve on the Supreme Court of the USA. She's one of the top judges in the US and she still feels like this.

Number two: Maya Angelou, a poet and writer who has spoken at Bill Clinton's inauguration, at rallies for Barack Obama, and is the recipient of a Pulitzer Prize nomination and three Grammys, and the first black woman to be shown on a quarter.

Number three: Emma Watson, actor, UN Women Goodwill Ambassador, activist for environmental justice, recipient of three MTV Movie Awards.

Do these women seem under-qualified to you?

Imposter syndrome is the experience of feeling like a phony in some area of your life, even if you are very successful. Merriam-Webster provides a succinct definition: it's "persistent doubt concerning one's abilities or accomplishments accompanied by the fear of being exposed as a fraud despite evidence of one's ongoing success." It's often linked to perfectionism. Commonly, people suffering from imposter syndrome feel as if they don't 'really' belong, as if their skills are just 'book learning' and not real, or as if they will get 'found out.' They feel like frauds. They don't feel comfortable in the positions of power and influence that they've reached.

Imposter syndrome can affect anyone. It's not a diagnosable mental illness, but it's a common perceptual bias. At least 70% of people will have feelings of imposter syndrome at some point in their lives, but some of those people will have more continuous feelings which affect them more severely. And it seems from research that imposter syndrome affects women much more than it does men. It affects women of color even more. And it is one of the major causes holding women back from leadership roles.

KPMG polled 750 high-performing, executive women, just a couple of steps away from the C-suite, who had participated in the KPMG Women's Leadership Summit. The results were surprising. Seventy-five percent of these women reported having experienced imposter syndrome during their career. Eighty-five percent believed it's commonly experienced by women in corporate America, and 74% believed men don't experience it to the same extent as women.

Eighty-one percent of these women also said they believe they put more pressure on themselves not to fail than men do ('not to fail,' rather than 'to succeed,' is an interesting emphasis).

They often fall into one of a small number of psychological impasses:

- The perfectionist trap: this woman believes that unless she's absolutely perfect, she could and should have done better. She has to be a perfect mother, perfect boss, perfect employee, *and* perfect person, or she is a failure.

- The expert trap: this woman believes that because she doesn't know *everything* about a subject, she doesn't really know anything about it.

- The natural genius trap: this woman takes time to master a skill and makes mistakes a few times before she gets the hang of it. She believes that because she doesn't get new things right first time, she's an imposter, or stupid.

- The soloist trap: this woman believes that if she couldn't get something done on her own, she's not really competent.

- The superperson trap: this woman believes she'll have to make superhuman effort to get to the top – the hardest worker, the student with the best exam results – and if she doesn't, she must be a fraud.

Do you recognize any of those symptoms? I suspect most of us recognize more than one!

Imposter syndrome, race and gender

Why does imposter syndrome affect women more than men? Partly, it's because of the absence of role models. Men see male leaders all around them: male CEOs, male presidents, male politicians and prime ministers, men running charities and foundations. Women don't see female role models nearly as often. That means a woman's concept of a 'leader' might be modeled on those male leaders, so there's something deep in her mind that doesn't understand how a woman can be a leader.

Look at the statistics and you see just how few good role models there are. Women are less likely to be hired and promoted; despite progress in the board room, they don't have anywhere near equal representation. France has the most women on corporate boards but even there, women are in the minority, with 44% of directorships. In the UK, women make up under a third of directors, and in the US only just over a quarter.

Black, indigenous and other people of color have even more difficulty finding role models in their fields (fortunately, the next generation of girls should find things have changed). Emily Hu, a Los Angeles psychologist, says "We're more likely to experience imposter syndrome if we don't see many examples of people who look like us or share our background who are clearly succeeding in our field."

Racist and sexist stereotypes cause marginalized people to doubt themselves. For instance, there's a stereotype that women are bad at math. One top class female accountant I know told me she'd always been 'bad at math,' though she was in the top quartile in her school – not being in the top *decile* meant, for her, she was 'bad' at the subject. She's anything but! Other stereotypes that can lead to self-doubt are:

- Women are 'too emotional' to make good leaders.
- POC are 'lazy' or 'undisciplined.'
- Women are not 'tough enough' to take hard decisions.

Even worse, many women are given the impression when they're young that they're only valued for being cute or pretty, and this can continue into adulthood. When they finally break into a profession, they keep asking themselves whether they were just hired for a pretty face. Some will also think they only got the job as a token woman or token black woman to fill a quota of diversity and equality in the workplace.

Recognizing and dealing with imposter syndrome

Recognizing imposter syndrome

Recognizing imposter syndrome is not hard. Self-doubt is a big piece of imposter syndrome. Do you always worry about whether you've got what it takes? Attributing your success to external factors is another characteristic behavior of people with imposter syndrome: "I was just in the right place at the right time" or "I was just lucky," they say, rather than "I deserved that promotion" or "I got that analysis right."

Imposter syndrome can mean you don't put yourself forwards, which is really difficult to deal with when you need to network or when you're running your own business. It can mean you don't understand why you've been nominated for an award: you don't feel your achievements can possibly be enough to deserve it.

Or you might agonize over the tiniest mistakes, like a single misspelt word in a report. You might be very defensive when faced with criticism, as if a single criticism means your whole career has been ruined; and yet you might also find it very difficult to accept praise. You might find yourself downplaying your expertise when in fact you're more skilled than other members of your team. You may feel under huge pressure to achieve; you may feel unable to ask for support in case people find out you've been faking it for years. You may also feel socially anxious – generally, or simply in work situations. This can be particularly the case for those of us who have to switch mode between a family or neighborhood situation and the way we speak at work.

Maureen Zappala, a mechanical engineer and now a well-known speaker on imposter syndrome, says, "For years I thought NASA only hired me because they needed women." She spent fourteen years on jet engine research and she still didn't quite believe she was qualified to do it.

Overcoming imposter syndrome

It's going to be hard to get past imposter syndrome. You have to take on board some tough questions and fight your inner critic and realize that the skills you can bring to the workplace are just as valuable as those that men or other women bring. Do you believe you're a worthwhile person? Do you believe you're worthy of love and respect just the way you are? Do you believe you have to be perfect for anyone to care about you or your opinion? What are your core beliefs about yourself? You're going to need to confront some deeply ingrained beliefs.

Some women will work with a therapist, particularly if their imposter syndrome stems from a conflicted family environment in their childhood that might have left them with other issues to face. But you can also confront your imposter syndrome quite successfully on your own.

First, be brave enough to share your feelings, perhaps with a partner or friend or mentor. Talking about those feelings can help put them into perspective. You might also sit down with a piece of paper and assess your skills rationally – things that you can do, situations you have dealt with, qualifications you have gained. You may be surprised by the difference between the person you see on paper and the person your negative thoughts suggest you are.

Now take baby steps forward. You don't have to do everything at once. For example, if you run your own business, you might say, "Once every day, when someone asks me what I do, I'm going to sound enthusiastic and confident and say I run my own business and this is what it does." Or you might put yourself forwards for a project role a little bit outside your comfort zone, or to head up a project in an area where you're well qualified.

Don't compare yourself with others. And don't listen to the negative voice of your inner critic – question it. If it says "You're not qualified," don't accept that; ask "What do I need to be qualified?" The answer may be that you don't need anything more than you already have.

The inner critic is unhelpful. So is the inner perfectionist. I don't mean you should become slapdash or not care about what you do, just that you shouldn't beat yourself up for tiny errors or omissions. You might be thinking all day about the fact that you forgot someone's name, and yet they didn't even notice! That's the inner critic, and that voice is distracting you from all the other things you should be focusing on. So, know what is good enough.

Identify allies and advocates in your workplace who believe in you. They'll be able to support you professionally but also personally. Check in with other women or maybe others who share your background and may share some of your difficulties in fully accepting their professional selves. Share ideas and advice with each other.

Join networking groups to help build your confidence in group settings. Pick groups that are related to your career interests. Seek out women in leadership roles; this will help you see that many women are doing great work.

Pay attention to your language choices. Do you often start off by saying "Sorry, but...?" Do you avoid expressing confidence? You need to stop doing that! Claim your expertise. Say things like "I think I should be able to deliver that," "Yes, I can handle complex statistical analysis," "Yes, I'm sure" (unless, *realistically*, you know that this isn't true. In which case, know what you need: more training, more resources, or not to do that job).

By the way, don't confuse the "Sorry but" reflex with humility, and don't think you have to deny your own success to give credit to your team. Being humble is about not bragging, not putting yourself above other people, listening to others and relating to them as equals – it's not about talking yourself down.

Catch those negative thoughts at source and challenge them. "You're a failure" – think about what you have actually achieved. "I was just lucky" – think about the work you put in, the judgments you made. You can even transform those challenges into affirmations such as "I worked hard; I'm a hard worker," or "I worked that out; I'm a real problem-solver."

Create an achievements file or 'brag file' on your computer. Include everything that you have been proud of throughout your career. Save emails that praise you, save certificates from training courses, awards, good feedback from colleagues, your glowing annual review. A thank you card from a client; get it in there. A great idea you had at a team meeting or someone you coached in your team. Look at that folder from time to time to see the reality of your success. And look for objective ways to measure your accomplishments, such as sales figures, efficiency ratios, or other metrics. Keep a diary of daily accomplishments and use a Kanban board or a focused to-do list – it really helps your confidence when you can cross off the things you've achieved. And of course, if you're feeling low, you can look at your 'brag file' to remind yourself that actually, you're a powerhouse of strength and skills. It's also a great tool to take to meetings if you're looking to progress (maybe head of department is your next goal).

And say "yes" to new opportunities. Get out of your comfort zone. Take a temporary job sorting out a crisis in a particular department, a training course. Take every opportunity you see. If you meet someone who can help you forwards in an area you may need to improve, take the bold step and ask them to help, instead of just thinking about it.

Become an expert. Chances are you are already great at some things in your job. Focus on a few areas and become an expert, become the go-to person in your company on this topic. And don't just stick to your comfort zone; remember that all the magic happens when you step outside of this. Become an expert in something that scares you. I have always been scared of public speaking. I would worry about it when someone told me I had to present until it was over. Over the years, I have purposely put myself in a position where I have to speak in public; at first, I did this in informal settings, which helped me gain confidence for when I had to do it in a more formal setting. I am not saying I now have no fear, but I am a lot better than I used to be and I definitely don't worry about it for weeks before. Are there any fears you can confront?

Focus on building confident behaviors. There is a famous saying – "fake it until you make it!" Practicing confident behaviors now will help you grow into a confident woman. Talk up in meetings. Push yourself outside of your comfort zone. If you are shy around new people, when you meet with people you have never met before, turn up early and start a conversation.

Take a more assertive tone, stand up straight, have confidence in yourself. It'll soon become habit.

Stop comparing yourself to other people on social media (you do know that when friends post holiday photos with turquoise seas and blue skies, they're using a photo filter, right?). A bit less social media use is probably a wise idea for many of us!

Start to connect with your inner self. What makes you unique? Many women do not take the time to really know themselves. Don't fall into the trap of thinking that you do not have as much to offer as others do; think about the facets of your personality that only you have and can share with others. Think about your hobbies or sport that you love. Maybe you have traveled a lot like I have and have seen and experienced many different cultures that make you a much more rounded person, able to see things from many different points of view and have a great appreciation of things that others may not. How do you spend your time and what do you value? Understand what interesting traits you can bring to the table; they could be a great asset to you and your company.

Know that you're not alone. Everyone feels apprehension and, sometimes, fear. Often the person in the room who looks happiest networking is the one who really, really hated being 'social' and making small talk; they *had* to learn how to look confident. Everyone (even men) feels a little twinge of worry the first time they walk into a new job. It's just the way it is.

Almost three quarters of executive women have asked for help from a mentor or trusted advisor to help overcome imposter syndrome. You are definitely not alone: you're in the vast majority. And just like the high-powered execs who reported feeling imposter syndrome, your feeling of worry has nothing at all to do with the reality of your being a successful female leader.

You may still *feel* like an imposter from time to time. But just stop imposter syndrome from stopping you doing worthwhile things. Regard it as a nay-saying old uncle, part of your family, quite a nice chap really, but he *will* keep nagging you... and then ignore it.

OVERCOMING IMPOSTER SYNDROME

- Challenge your inner critic
- Work with a therapist
- Be brave enough to share your feelings with others
- Assess your skills rationally
- Don't compare yourself with others
- Don't beat yourself up for tiny errors
- Identify allies and advocates in the workplace who believe in you
- Join networking groups to build confidence
- Don't use negative language choices
- Catch negative thoughts and challenge them
- Create a brag file to look back on
- Say "yes" to new opportunities
- Become an expert in a few areas
- Focus on building confident behaviors
- Stop comparing yourself to others on social media
- Connect with your inner self
- Remember that you're not alone in these feelings

Help your team avoid imposter syndrome

Imposter syndrome isn't helpful to your team. Individuals suffering imposter syndrome may not be performing at their peak, or they may be highly stressed while delivering their contribution. They may be afraid to take on new challenges, and they may be unreceptive to change.

Do you see other people who might be struggling with the same feelings that you have? Having a supportive workplace can make a big difference. Highly competitive workplaces where team members are forced to compete against each other can make the problem worse, as can organizations which have unclear objectives or 'unwritten rules,' or which lack diversity.

If you provide mentoring, that will help support your team members. If you have open communications, clear targets, and a relaxed workplace, that will also help. You might want to discuss feelings of discomfort, self-doubt, and perfectionism openly, perhaps at the same time as you talk about personal and career development plans. Sometimes, people are suffering from imposter syndrome without ever having realized that 'it's a thing' – they think it's just them.

A culture of inclusion helps team members speak up without fearing other people will be dismissive or patronizing. Don't allow interruptions and make sure everyone has equal time to speak. Ensure they take their opportunity to speak, too: learn to ask questions to get them going, if they don't come forward.

Recognizing a team member's effort, not just their achievement, will help them feel valid and valued. "You worked really hard on this" is a great thing to say if you want to keep imposter syndrome at bay.

Training and development plans for every member of the team should address what they feel are weak points, but you should also coach them through learning new skills. Remember that confidence is a learned skill! If you have a team member who is stuck in their comfort zone, don't give them a big challenge and let them fail – give them a small step, then another, till they are ready to take on a bigger challenge.

Step Four
KNOW YOUR LEADERSHIP STYLE AND MAKE CHANGES WHERE NECESSARY

No one quite agrees how to break leadership down. However, the last twenty years in management research have seen a number of attempts to tackle this issue, and one of the most convincing, I think, comes from Jim Kouzes and Barry Posner, who developed what they define as the 'Five Practices of Exemplary Leadership':

1. Model the way – put up signposts, set directions.

2. Inspire shared vision – use imagination as well as targets.

3. Challenge the process – don't accept the status quo.

4. Enable others to act – empower others, create effective teams.

5. Encourage the heart – mutual respect, integrity, caring.

Not everyone does these things the same way, and different leaders strike different balances between those five aspects. You'll develop your own leadership style over time, and in line with your own personality, your values, strengths, abilities, and experiences.

Some people define up to seventeen different styles of leadership. However, it's more usual to look at seven or eight. I think the first three in this list are quite difficult to develop into leadership, though; they're often used by people who are natural bosses or managers, not leaders. Be very careful if you are using these styles; you may need to develop towards one of the other styles as you progress in your career.

Try not to lead like a man. To be an effective leader, you must embrace who you really are. Do you find yourself taking on more masculine traits to try and fit in? Overly risky, demanding or harassing, or belittling behaviors are linked to toxic masculinity. Stop caring about fitting in, about whether people like you as a leader. Part of your role will be making unpopular decisions from time to time. Often this is challenging because we are preconditioned to want to be liked. But a great leader needs to balance these qualities with the larger needs of the business. Work on getting comfortable with being uncomfortable, as you'll soon learn to ride the rough with the smooth.

As a leader, you will be expected to assume roles in different capacities, given your situation. An understanding of the key leadership styles can help you fine-tune your approach according to the circumstances. You'll need to be aware of the weaknesses of each style and focus on the strengths if you want to create a strong team. Let's look at some of these.

Leadership styles

Transactional leadership

This can be summed up in the Latin phrase 'do ut des,' which describes the exchange the Romans expected when making a sacrifice to the gods: I give you this, so you'll do that for me. This leadership style is usually highly directive, using carrots and sticks, work packages and deadlines. It can be effective, and it can also be comfortable for a team which knows exactly what's expected, but you run the risk of getting satisficing behavior from the team ('good enough' performance rather than that which goes the extra mile) and suppressing innovation and creativity.

Example: Bill Gates started out this way; however, he later developed his style to give employees more autonomy.

Autocratic leadership

The leader with absolute power. This tends to be a male leadership style, though some women use it too. Many small business owners are like this; because they own the business, they don't have to accept anyone's advice. They hire and fire, they micromanage, they tell their employees what to do and how to do it. If they're perceptive and smart, they'll meet their objectives, but employees won't be happy and probably won't do their best. And they'll never know how much better the business might have been if team members had felt able to contribute their ideas (again, I'd call this 'being a boss' and not 'leadership').

Examples include: Steve Jobs, Donald Trump, Martha Stewart.

Bureaucratic leadership

This is a type that a lot of women adapt easily to. They take their power from the organizational structure, so they don't need to feel like a powerful personality themselves to lead their team. The processes, procedures, systems, tasks and goals are clear. There's no need for risk taking, no need to stick your neck out. If you're running a franchise, bureaucratic leadership can help achieve standardization across your franchises. On the plus side, most people like the stability of working in this kind of environment, but the big negative is that you're likely to suppress innovation.

Examples include: Steve Easterbrook at McDonald's; Alfred P. Sloan at GM.

Laissez-faire leadership

This borrows a French phrase that literally translates as "let you do" and it means letting people just get on with the job. It's a really hands-off approach. A laissez-faire leader will make the vision clear and provide tools and resources, but then they'll step back. It's the reverse of micro-management. It's a style that goes down well in IT and other professional teams, where team members are highly skilled and motivated or very experienced. Employees aren't bogged down by feedback and are encouraged to use creativity and make their own decisions which is great for moral but can lead to conflict where there is no guidance and team members disagree on approach.

A lack of support can undermine some team members, and if you don't put work into building a strong team first, you may end up with people working against rather than with each other.

Example: Warren Buffett – he buys companies and lets good management get on with running them.

Charismatic leadership

From the outside, this can look like autocratic leadership, since both autocrats and charismatic leaders possess strong personalities. But charismatic leaders use persuasion and vision to excite and motivate their teams. They're great public speakers and make great figureheads for their companies or causes. But they can be so focused that they risk 'believing their own PR' and not noticing changes in the business environment, or not giving due weight to input from members of the team.

Examples include: Richard Branson, Martin Luther King.

Participative leadership

Participative leadership or 'democratic' leadership emphasises working *together* and actively involving the team in decision-making. Collaborating and asking for others' input makes team members feel valued and inspires creativity and high performance. On the other hand, getting a decision made can be time-consuming, and this isn't always a great leadership style if you're dealing with a crisis.

A lot of leaders best known for other styles use a lot of participative leadership too, particularly when they have built a team they really trust and have grown their business together with that team.

Example: Jack Ma, CEO of Alibaba.

Servant leadership

This is about service first and leadership second. The servant leader prioritizes other people's needs. It's a style that's often found in social enterprises and charities. Servant leaders will try to help out, to remove roadblocks, and to give their employees confidence. The risk is that if you don't have a strong vision, you'll be seen as a patsy rather than a leader.

Examples include: Nelson Mandela, the Dalai Lama.

Transformational leadership

This aims to inspire employees to innovate and create, and to transform themselves and the business. Transformational leaders empower other people, give them autonomy, are receptive to feedback, and take risks. They're happy to go outside their comfort zones, and they expect others to do the same. This style of leadership can get great results, but you need to ensure team members get enough support to deal with the pace of change.

Most great leaders of disruptive companies and turnarounds are transformational leaders. They may have started with or lean toward other styles but know that they need to get out of those comfort zones to really move forward.

Get to know your leadership style. This will help you personally, as you can clearly see the advantages and disadvantages of the style. For instance, if you know you're a fairly transactional leader, you may decide to use more 'carrot' and less 'stick' to keep your team motivated. Or you may want to use a mix of leadership styles. Good leaders will flex between styles depending on the situation they're in and the people they're dealing with; this will become easier with practice.

It can also help colleagues if you can articulate the way you lead. For instance, sometimes other leaders in your organization may think you're 'not actually managing' the team if you have a participative or laissez faire style. You need to be able to explain the way you keep the team moving forward, if it's not the same as the way others manage. Of course, it can also be helpful to explain your management style to team members so they know what to expect.

Be aware that it's easy to clash with those who prefer other leadership styles. A colleague who likes a structured work environment where they always know exactly what they need to do may not find it easy to adjust to working in a collaborative team with a participative or transformational leader. They'll need helping to get outside their comfort zone. Equally, if you have a more transactional style, you may find some of the more innovative members of your team start to display some frustration at having what they consider too much structure (consider making part of your 'contract' that they spend 10% of their time on innovation).

Incorporating each style in the workplace

Transactional leadership

Transactional leadership can work well for regulated industries or in manufacturing, and in multinational businesses where policies and procedures help standardize across cultures and languages. It also works well in areas where employees are likely to be motivated by rewards, for example, in sales, where staff are likely to be highly motivated by bonuses and commissions.

For transactional leadership to work well, you need to ensure everybody is absolutely clear about their goals and targets. You'll also need to earn their trust that if they reach those targets, you will give them that reward. And you need to always communicate very openly and honestly to gain their loyalty.

Transactional leaders can work very quickly in a crisis or to achieve a turnaround; they don't need to discuss things or reach a consensus, or to convince employees of their vision. They can simply take charge. So, if you use this style, you can afford to take certain risks.

Autocratic leadership

Back in the nineteenth century, most people thought autocratic leadership was the only way to get results. Nowadays, it tends to have rather a bad reputation. But it does work in certain conditions. If you learn how to use it wisely, you'll have an extra weapon to use in a crisis or in other situations it may be needed.

For instance, in a small group, where egos are becoming a problem, or different agendas are making agreement impossible, an autocratic leader can take charge and push the project forward. An autocratic leader may also be needed to take charge of a rookie team where none of the team members have much experience.

People who gravitate towards autocratic leaders often seek guidance, so these leaders can guide people to achieve great things where needed. They are generally adaptable and will get to know each team member individually. Their reliability and trustworthiness can be great for team morale. But they need to ensure that their hands-on approach does not lead to micro-management.

Autocratic leaders also do well in crisis situations, where tight deadlines have to be met, and in dangerous situations or those where things absolutely have to be done perfectly, for instance in surgery or aircraft maintenance. If you're usually a participative leader, but you suddenly become an autocrat, most teams will realize what that means: the chips are down; things are serious; you've got to get the job done, perfectly, and right now.

Bureaucratic leadership

There are some major advantages to bureaucratic leadership. It's impersonal; egos and personal styles don't get in the way of carrying out the job. Everyone knows what they need to do and how to do it. In regulated industries, it's important to show that due process has been followed – for instance, in personal finance, that you've complied with money laundering and 'know your client' regulations – so bureaucratic leadership can be useful in helping demonstrate this.

More skilled employees may find bureaucratic leadership dull, but it's a good way to manage inexperienced staff. It also avoids favoritism and infighting, since the procedures for work assessment and promotion are clear.

Laissez-faire leadership

Laissez-faire leadership might look to some people like doing nothing. In fact, if you want to succeed with laissez-faire leadership, you need some serious soft skills and there is a lot of work you'll need to do with your team and individual team members.

For instance, to let people 'just get on with it,' you need to be an active listener. Otherwise, you'll miss people's insights, and you may also miss their coded appeals for help. "Well, it's not going quite as well as it was" may actually mean "We're losing a lot of deals and we don't know why." You can then help them address the issue by asking them the right questions, and providing support where it's needed, but *they* will decide how to solve the problem.

You need to be good at asking questions. You might ask: "How can we make you more productive?" for instance, if someone isn't able to handle all their action points, or "What would you need to be able to double sales?" if you think targets could be more aggressive. You're aiming to stimulate the team to work out how to do it for themselves.

You also need to make sure your vision is understood by the team. For instance, Warren Buffett is able to practice laissez-faire leadership with the companies he owns, because he has a very clearly expressed philosophy of prioritizing long-term shareholder value, not short-term returns, and his senior executives all understand it.

Charismatic leadership

Many charismatic leaders look egotistical. Their brand is all about them – their enthusiasm, their vision, their objectives. But you actually need to mix in a good dose of humility for it to work really well. You need to listen to your team and keep channels open to everyone in the organization;

otherwise, you may not hear what they're saying, because you're too busy talking.

Mahatma Gandhi was one of the most charismatic leaders of the twentieth century. Unlike many, he espoused non-violence, and he refused to command anyone to perform any action. He simply did things himself and let people follow.

If you're a charismatic leader, it's up to you to keep people's energy high. You need to ensure you are always upbeat, even when addressing challenges and failures. Reframe negative events by asking what can be done about them. That can be hard when you're feeling less than confident yourself, so you'll need to reach right down to your core for the belief and energy that you need.

Participative leadership

Participative leadership is good when you're working with skilled and experienced people, and when you have the luxury of time – when you can concentrate on the long term. It's great for inspiring creativity, and it's also the best way to manage millennials, who have certain expectations about how they should be treated.

You'll need to make it clear to your team what you want to achieve, and that you want their feedback in order to achieve it. For instance, if you were organizing a project team including builders, architects and town planners to 'make New York greener,' you'd need to have defined what success would look like – more green space, lower energy use, or maybe less waste going to landfill?

You'll then want to spend some time talking about how you're going to collaborate. Will there be regular meetings? How will decisions get made? Are you aiming for a consensus or a majority vote? How do you ensure everyone is listened to? Will there be different phases, for instance brainstorming, idea selection, and feasibility study?

If you want participative leadership to work, you have to put the work in upfront.

Servant leadership

Becoming a servant leader starts by setting an example. A servant leader will never ask a member of the team to do anything they wouldn't do themselves. A servant leader will also never let a member of the team go without support. Think of the number of officers who have been awarded medals for gallantry because they ran back into fire to carry out wounded soldiers.

Show your team you care about them as people, not just as workers. If they have issues with work-life balance, ask how you can help. Share your personal experiences with them if you think it might help: "I had problems giving presentations at first. Then I learned that sometimes you can take catch a breath when you change slide; let people refocus; you don't have to talk all the time. It took the pressure off."

Ask for feedback. And give it: "Hey, that was a great presentation!" Encourage members of the team to collaborate and work together with each other to achieve more.

But above all, make sure your team know that they're there to make a difference, whatever they're doing right now. You may be selling tickets for an exhibition of women's art, but if the proceeds go towards educating girls in countries where female learning is not a priority, you're changing lives.

Transformational leadership

To start implementing transformational leadership, you'll need to start work with yourself. You'll need to develop charisma – and yes, it can be developed. For some people, taking up a mindfulness practice and just feeling more grounded can help develop confidence and charisma. You'll also develop your own style – remember Steve Jobs' iconic black turtleneck?

You may also need to develop your empathy. Some of us are more people-oriented than others. If your background is very task-oriented, you may need to start taking time to get to know members of your team on a personal level. Journal ten minutes every day if that's what it takes to get you going. Understand the personal goals your team members are working towards, what are the things they worry about, what really gets them motivated. You may find it difficult at first, but the more you practice, the better you get.

Then you'll need to create the proper culture in your workplace. You'll need to encourage collaboration, whether that means creating project teams to replace a bureaucratic structure, or simply creating reporting structures that let individuals see clearly how their work feeds into the group result. You'll also need great communication. If team members have previously worked for a boss who didn't encourage feedback, they may feel hesitant at first. You'll need to make a real effort to show their input is valued.

Finally, you'll need to have a real grasp of the core values and goal of your organization. If you don't have that, you may have the skills to transform it, but you don't have any vision of what you want it to be.

Leadership style	Traits	How to incorporate it into your role
Transactional	Carrot and stick Deadlines Highly directive	Works well where motivated by reward Ensure goals and targets are clear Use in a crisis
Autocratic	Leader with power Micro-management	Use to take charge and move projects forward Use in crisis situations with tight deadlines

Leadership style	Traits	How to incorporate it into your role
Bureaucratic	Lead alongside organizational structure Minimal risk taking	Good way to manage inexperienced staff Show that due process has been followed
Laissez-faire	Giving employees autonomy Hands off leadership	Use your soft skills Be an active listener Ask open ended questions
Charismatic	Strong personality Persuasion and vision	Show enthusiasm and vision Keep energy high
Participative	Emphasises working together Getting input from others	Make clear goals Get regular feedback
Servant	Prioitize other people's needs Lack of strong vision	Set an example Be supportive Show your employees you care Communicate they're making a difference

Leadership style	Traits	How to incorporate it into your role
Transformational	Inspire employees to innovate Risk taking	Develop charisma Show empathy Get to know your employees on a personal level Develop company culture well Encourage collaboration Great communication

You can't fix everything

People often expect the leader to do everything for them. They think their leader should know everything, should do everything, should be everything. From fixing the lightbulbs to knowing the details of competitive products, from motivating the team to monitoring the budget, they think it's the leader's job, and they're disappointed if their leader says: "I can't do that," or "you'll have to ask Finance," or "maybe you should find that out."

Worse, some leaders take this on board. They think they should be able to fix everything. They become 'the fixer,' and they judge themselves against this ludicrous standard. Women in particular tend to do this, because they have a separate set of expectations imposed on them by society – to be a great mom, a loving wife, *and* a chief executive, to 'do it all' and do it perfectly. Then they end up feeling like miserable failures because there's just one thing they can't do, whether it's a networking event, a school football game, or having perfect grooming every single day.

So, you need to take on your 'inner fixer,' as leadership writer Lolly Daskal says. You need to stop believing you have to do everything. You may need to face down voices from your childhood, from teachers or former bosses or from the media, that tell you how you need to be responsible for everyone, to be able to answer every question. You may even need to deal with those demons who tell you that you'll be a failure if you can't. This can be difficult, and it may take time.

You also need to learn to trust other people to take charge of their own lives and tasks. Rather than trying to solve their problems, learn to ask questions that will help them decide what to do, and then offer support if it's still required.

Watch out for situations where, without noticing, you end up having made yourself totally responsible for a problem. You start by helping with one issue, and before you know it, you've been swallowed up. This is what Lolly Daskal calls "emotional hostage syndrome" and it's a clear sign that you need to take a step back. You need to regain perspective.

Micro-management

We have already touched on micro-management – it is similar to the 'fixer' syndrome. Micro-managers try to control every detail of their employees' work: how, where and when they do it, and how they take decisions. For instance, most managers who have asked an employee to write up a report or make slides for a presentation will brief them clearly, then leave them to get on with the first draft. But a micro-manager will keep asking where the employee has got to, how it's coming along, and whether they still expect to get it done on time. Micro-managers are control freaks.

If the report is good, most managers will maybe discuss a couple of nuances in the introduction or conclusion. They might ask for a topic to be expanded a little, or a new topic to be included. A micro-manager will go through and correct the spelling and grammar, ask for a different font to be used, and complain that they asked for a thirty-page report and only got twenty-nine pages.

You've probably been micro-managed at some point in your career and if so, you know how demoralizing it can be. You don't feel trusted to get on with the job. Creativity disappears and employees concentrate on doing exactly what the micro-manager requires, rather than bringing their own ideas to the task. Micro-managers aren't good for morale, but they're not good for the organization either, because they can't see the wood for the trees (who cares about the spelling when a report is making the wrong recommendation?). The effects of micro-management can run rampant through an organization and destroy its culture, leading to high turnover rates and increased sick time.

Often, micro-management stems from fear of inadequacy. Managers are afraid that one of their employees will make a mistake and they won't catch it. In some cases, they've been promoted to head up a team they previously worked in, and they haven't made the emotional adjustment to step up to their new job. Some also want to communicate more with their employees, but they don't have the social skills to do so in a more useful way than micro-managing.

So, if you're starting to micro-manage, how do you stop?

First of all, divide what your team is doing into the really important stuff and the unimportant (we will look at how you can do this in more detail later when we look at the Eisenhower matrix in step seven). The order in which someone does their tasks (unless it affects project dependencies) isn't important, nor is the format of a spreadsheet (unless it has to fit a standard accounting format for the company or it is being sent to a client). Vow not to bother about the unimportant stuff. Leave it alone!

Secondly, if your staff don't have clear performance goals, you need to create a set of goals that you can monitor. Exactly what are they expected to do? Meet with each employee to ensure they fully understand the goals and offer them support if they need it at any point. Then set them free to achieve their goals. Don't monitor what they're doing at any one time; you don't need to, as you will be monitoring the outcome.

Don't hover. If you find this difficult, actually set your watch, and measure the length of time you leave your staff without 'checking in' – then double it. Creating some physical distance can help, whether that's working on another site one day a week, closing the office door occasionally, or letting team members work at home.

Most employees will gladly work independently, coming to you when they are unsure about the exact route to take, or find there's a roadblock that may need your authority to remove. A few employees won't. It's probably those ones that you worry about. You feel that if you don't keep on top of them, they won't bother working. But you already gave them clear goals; if they don't get to grips with the new way of working, perhaps they shouldn't be working for you.

Do, though, give your employees the chance to give you feedback. Some employees, particularly younger or less confident team members, may want you to manage them more actively and feel a bit lost without regular input. Others may be happy to be independent but don't want to feel you are 'remote' or 'aloof.' Ask them how often they'd like to check in, and how much support they think they need.

Stopping micro-managing can be tough at first, so you need to remind yourself that you're a leader, and there are things that only you can do: motivating the team, developing your team members, establishing the way forward. Think hard about the things you do that really make a difference, and then look at micro-managing activities and the lack of value they add.

Step Five
BUILD SELF-CONFIDENCE IN YOURSELF AND YOUR TEAM

E ven without imposter syndrome, many women lack confidence at work. Sometimes that can be because you need skills that you don't yet have, or you're the least experienced member of your team, or you've moved to a new company and you're still trying to understand the new culture and get used to it. You might have an overbearing or obnoxious colleague. Or you might have just made a bad mistake and be trying to live it down.

Most often, though, the reason for low self-confidence is a poor relationship with the boss. Negative peer relationships can also damage self-confidence, and that can be a problem for the whole team. Sometimes, a 'pack' mentality leads to a particular group feeling threatened and trying to undermine other team members. That can happen, for example, when a fresh graduate is brought into a team where most of the members learned on the job, or when an outsider is brought into a team which is 'home grown.'

The good news is that as you progress towards leadership and or take a leadership role, you can ensure good relationships with your team, and you can also help to ensure your team avoids internal problems.

Why confidence is a women's issue

Dr Russ Harris coined the term 'the confidence gap' to explain why women appear to have less confidence than men. For instance, a study at Hewlett-Packard found that men applied for a job if they met 60% of the qualifications and experience needed, women only if they had 100%. The confidence gap, among other things, explains why women tend to outperform men academically, but then start to underperform once they join the workforce.

There are several reasons for this. One reason is biological: men have 10% higher levels of testosterone than women. This increases their risk-taking behavior and their confidence. It will also make the individual appear more ambitious and 'driven' in a corporate world which tends to value those qualities.

But a lot of the difference comes from the different ways boys and girls are brought up. Boys are more often allowed to be loud, to engage in robust physical behavior and even fight; they're encouraged to be resilient. Girls, on the other hand, are often expected to be quiet and gentle, and aren't encouraged to express themselves physically. Peer pressure can also encourage young women to refrain from speaking or 'acting up' and to downplay their intelligence. Women find it difficult to take up space; they may even try to make themselves look physically smaller, adopting contained body language that suggests submission or low self-confidence; they fear being seen as 'overbearing' or 'too dominant' (one colleague reported that when she spoke up at a meeting, one man said loudly: "You can see who wears the trousers in her house").

Women don't just behave differently; they internalize this behavior. Employer branding specialist Universum surveyed UK students recently and found that 41% of male business students, but only 34% of females, described themselves as high performers. The male students also had salary expectations 12% higher than female students. This isn't a huge gap, but it widens with seniority, instead of narrowing.

Enabling women to be more confident is a win for the women involved. But it's also a big win for the employer. Having a confident workforce impresses customers. A lot of the time, women spend their time trying hard to be modest in the fear that otherwise, they won't be likeable. However, it may have the effect of making others feel they are not talented or qualified at their jobs, instead.

Having a confident workforce is also likely to enable every staff member to put forward their ideas to improve the organization. Lack of confidence stops employees from performing and can mean they are not fully engaged. And if you look confident, you'll attract the right individuals to work on your team, as they will feel you're the kind of boss who will be successful. Confident workers also represent your brand best. One reason the concierge at a luxury hotel is so important is that the concierge is the "I can fix that" person, and even if in reality they're panicking about getting someone tickets for a sold-out event, they *look* totally confident and make customers feel that they're being looked after by an infallible, all-competent and all-knowing genius. Giving customers that feeling is one way the hotel justifies its high price tag.

So as a leader, you need to build your own self-confidence, and you also need to help your staff feel confident and express their confidence in their work. Remember that women tend to blame themselves more; as a leader, you can help take at least some of that pressure off the women who work for (and with) you.

Developing self-confidence

Adopt a confident mindset

Help yourself develop your self-confidence by adopting a confident mindset. Focus on your strengths and on what you have achieved. Focus on positive feelings. If you catch negative thoughts coming into your mind, focus on a positive instead. "I might mess up my presentation" can be countered by "I really impressed my team when I rehearsed the presentation, so I will be able to do well in front of the board."

Tell yourself "I can do this" and believe in yourself. Before you go to bed, tell yourself three things that worked well for you today, three things you like or respect about yourself, or three things you worked hard on. Use affirmations. A good way to do that is to find something you did and then add the affirmation: "I got my team to work together at last. I'm a great team builder," or "I got a product launched. I'm efficient and productive!"

Start a confidence journal. Note quickly, at the end of the day, the things you did well, the challenges you took up, the times you went outside of your comfort zone. Give yourself a pat on the back for doing so. If you later feel unsure of yourself, look back at the confidence journal to see how well you did things in the past.

Try to be an optimist

Find happiness – whether that's in your family, your hobby or your friends – and show that in your work. We all know the kind of person who's always downbeat and never shows any enthusiasm for their work. That kind of person never makes a leader. Become a role model for positivity: find solutions for problems, show an upbeat attitude, and smile (if you want to see what positivity looks like, search for one of Gurdeep Pandher's videos – he's been dancing bhangra all the way round Canada to bring "joy, hope and positivity" to schools and communities).

Learn how to 'flip your thoughts' from negative to positive

For instance, "I'm not good enough" becomes "I can improve and I will." "I failed" becomes "this was a learning experience" – and note what you learned. Negative thoughts will always pop into your head, however confident you are; the difference is that confident people learn to be their own best friend. You know that if you tell your best friend that something was a disaster, they won't pile on you: "That just shows you're an idiot, you can't sing, you'll never amount to anything, you're stupid." Instead, they'll say "Look at it this way: you overcame your fear and got up there and did karaoke; it will never be that scary again," or "*my* first driving lesson was *way* worse than that!" Learn to be your own best friend and flip those negative thoughts.

Research has shown the power of affirmations in helping positivity. Instead of beating yourself up, tell yourself – "I am worthy, I am talented, I am strong." Spend ten minutes thinking of some affirmations that would be unique to you to help build your confidence and say these each morning or before you go to bed.

Use the right body language and posture

Get your posture right. Don't try to take up as little space as possible or shrink into the background. Stand tall and keep grounded. Feel your own weight going down through your feet into the ground (doing aikido, tai chi, or judo can really help you develop this feeling of groundedness). If you've heard of 'manspreading' – men taking up room on the subway by sitting with their elbows and knees out, squashing whoever's in the next seat – women tend to do the reverse, shrinking away. Instead, just take your space.

Try not to cross your arms, which makes you small as well as blocking off contact. Crossed arms say "no entry" and look unfriendly.

Make, and maintain, eye contact with whoever you are speaking to. If you're in a meeting and you want to address one person, make eye contact with them across the table.

Speak up in meetings

It's not easy, the first few times. Actively participate in discussion and remember to keep eye contact; don't look down at your papers. Speak clearly; don't mumble. Learn to project your voice (acting classes are great if you have problems here!). And don't be afraid of silence. If you ask "How can we get this done?" and no one answers for a few seconds, don't rush on; let the silence 'work.' Sooner or later, someone will say something.

Learn assertiveness

You'll be taken more seriously if you do. It's not the same as aggressiveness; it's about simply stating what you want or need, and making your voice heard. So, for instance, if someone talks over you, aggressiveness would be trying to shout them down; assertiveness is simply saying "I hadn't finished. Can you let me finish please?" To be assertive, you need to keep calm. If you feel that your voice is beginning to rise or you're beginning to feel too hot, that's a sure sign that you need to take a deep breath, and *then* assert yourself.

Don't get over-confident

Men often do. If you're asked to deliver a report on a highly complex area in just a couple of days, and you think that's unrealistic, don't try to bluff your way through. Don't assume you will learn everything you need to know about a new job in the first week. But at the same time, be prepared to go outside your comfort zone, to take on a target or task that makes you stretch a little.

Build on your strengths and try to extend your competences

Learn to project them through what you say and do. Discover what makes you exceptional and let that drive you. Ask people what they think are your greatest strengths – do they all agree? If they mention qualities that you didn't think were really your strengths, you may need to sit down and think about their feedback. Perhaps they're right! Or are people overlooking something that you consider a strength, perhaps because you don't use it much in your current role?

Use your strengths. Look for opportunities to maximize them. These strengths are your personal armory and your personal brand. Sometimes, other people see the talents you haven't yet discovered. Research has shown that people who focus on their strengths are more confident. You should aim to spend 80% of your time focusing on your strengths and 20% of your time focusing on the weaknesses that matter to your job; this will make you an all-rounder.

Identify and use your superpower

Don't just do your job adequately, but become known for your 'superpower.' That might be problem-solving, or it might be your ability to generate ideas, for instance. 'Lead from your strengths' and think about the opportunities your role gives you to use them and make the most of those chances.

Know your weaknesses

You might be able to eliminate or reduce them. Overcoming a small weakness can really boost your confidence. You might decide to take a training course on public speaking if it's an area where you feel shaky. You might also consider getting a mentor to help you with the areas where you feel weak or lack self-confidence. Remember the eighty/twenty rule.

Stay focused

Don't get caught up in playing office politics, or in rumours. Stay on-task.

Identify what your triggers are

Identify trigger situations which make your confidence suddenly flow away. We all have them: for some people, it's standing up on a stage; for others, it's having to come out with a definite number or to deal with someone else's strong emotions. Think about situations in which you feel confident, then about ones in which you feel at risk and fearful. Think about why this is, and what might change your feeling in the negative situations. Then next time you're in that situation, try to hold on to that knowledge, and navigate the situation a different and more confident way.

Challenge yourself

Every time you succeed in a challenge you will build your self-confidence one step more. Find assignments that stretch you, or projects which are demanding but where you can bring your strengths into play. Remember that it's okay to feel unsure or nervous, even afraid. Remember, if you are doing something new, don't compare yourself to someone who has been doing it for years; that would be like doing your first karaoke and comparing yourself to Madonna or Rod Stewart!

"Feel the fear and do it anyway" as Susan Jeffers says; take some risks. Learn to enjoy experimentation and risk-taking. For instance, challenge yourself in your personal life to try a different cuisine or a different sport every month, to try reading a book you always thought was too 'difficult' or to do something pleasantly scary, like playing paintball or riding the big dipper. And look around you if you do something scary, because you'll see clearly that you're not the only one feeling scared.

Give yourself permission to fail

At least at first – when you're really stretching. It isn't easy to get new things right first time, so don't judge yourself too early. Try to find safe spaces to practice things, such as trying out a presentation with a mentor or peer before you have to deliver it to the board. The first time you ask a question at a big conference, don't expect too much of yourself – just ask a simple question; next time you can ask something more interesting.

Expect to have your confidence knocked

Understand that your confidence will get a few knocks from time to time. A mean comment can really shake your confidence; try not to respond. Give yourself a couple of days to put it in perspective and get your confidence back. It can sometimes help to think about why that comment was made: was your colleague feeling threatened, or protecting their turf? Get your emotional radar working. When someone tries to give you a hard knock, it's not usually anything to do with your performance – it's not you, it's them.

DEVELOPING SELF-CONFIDENCE

- Adopt a confident mindset
- Try to be an optimist
- Learn how to 'flip your thoughts' from negative to positive

- Use the right body language and posture
- Speak up in meetings
- Learn assertiveness
- Don't get over-confident
- Build on your strengths
- Extend your competences
- Identify and use your superpower
- Know your weaknesses
- Stay focused
- Identify your triggers
- Challenge yourself
- Give yourself permission to fail
- Expect to have your confidence knocked

Developing confidence in your team

If you want to have a team that's more than an assortment of random people, you need to create confidence in each individual, and you also need to create confidence in the team as a whole. The first thing you'll need to do is to educate managers and team leaders about the confidence gap, and create an awareness that confidence is something that may need to be built; not everyone has it to start with, whichever gender they are.

Make your team a 'safe place' by insisting on constructive feedback, not negative criticism. In the theater, many directors employ trust exercises to ensure actors feel the rehearsal room is their 'safe space'; this can be vital when working on plays which address difficult issues or are emotionally challenging. As team leader, you can help by not trying to find people to blame when things go wrong but trying to learn from mistakes.

Establish inclusive ways to communicate. Ensure every member feels able to express their thoughts and feelings and is able to contribute to discussions. Be aware of who speaks the most, and who speaks the least; you may need to try to redress the balance in your meetings. Remember that secret agendas and in-groups destroy confidence and trust.

Help team members to "fail forward" – try to see failures as learning experiences. What could they have done differently? What skill or resource would have helped them do better? Can you help? Can another team member help?

Find your team members' strengths and help them play to their strengths by giving them jobs where that strength is going to be useful. If they're in the wrong role, find the right one for them. Help them to a win; set up your team members' success.

Learn to recognize team members who don't have enough self-confidence. Encourage them to learn, and to take small opportunities to expand their abilities. Start with small steps, supporting them every step of the way. For instance, sit with them while they're learning a new programming language or how to use a spreadsheet to budget. You can wean them off this support as they gain in skill and confidence.

Set them clear goals and remember they will need praise as well as a sense of achievement to boost their confidence when they meet those goals. Be specific in praise. "You solved that problem by being pragmatic and imaginative at the same time" or "Did you see how your questions helped people define the project better?" are good pieces of feedback and help your team member think back through the experience and understand what they did particularly well. Delegate properly and celebrate success.

Be prepared to share your own past experience. You might explore how you addressed certain trigger situations or recommend books that helped you. Remember, though, that if you're going to coach team members in confidence, you need to set that situation apart from 'normal' work. An appraisal, which is always a time of tension, is absolutely the wrong time to explore these issues. This coaching role might be better filled by a mentor than by you as team leader.

Above all, create a structure for learning within the team. Don't throw employees in at the deep end; give them a structured progression, including support and/or check-in sessions to ensure they're not struggling. If you're giving them a new role, talk about it, what it requires, how you could define and measure success, and what worries they may have, or what resources they might need. Have your team members teach each other, present to each other, share their skills or newly acquired knowledge and methods. You might even pair staff to work on some things, giving each new team member a more experienced employee who can help them take on a new role.

Step Six
MANAGE YOUR TIME EFFECTIVELY

Time management is important to anyone who has things to do. But it's particularly important if you are a leader, because you are likely to have more and a greater variety of tasks to accomplish than you did at a lower level. You have to look after your team and the individuals who are part of it, as well as being responsible for delivering your part of the enterprise's plan; you have to run the budgets as well as achieving your deliverables; and you'll also want to plan for some learning, and career and personal development.

So, time management is really crucial for you, and that's why I've devoted a whole chapter to it. If you are stretching yourself at the moment and missing out some aspects of your job, or your life, because there isn't enough time right now, let me tell you this: there never *will* be enough time.

What can better time management deliver for you? Let's just run off a quick list:

- Get more done with less effort and have more energy.
- Stop procrastinating.
- Focus more easily.

- Become more productive.
- Experience less stress.
- Have more time for your team.
- Have time to think deeply instead of rushing things.
- Make better thought-through decisions.
- Get less distracted.
- Achieve a better work/life balance.

I think that little list makes time management a worthwhile skill to learn. Don't you?

I talked earlier about distinguishing tasks by how important and how urgent they are. If you draw a four-box grid, you can make what's called an 'Eisenhower matrix'. The idea is credited to US President Dwight Eisenhower – not just a president, but an architect and leader of the successful operations in Normandy in World War II, so he knew all about taking decisions under time pressure.

Along the bottom, you mark 'urgent' for the first column and 'not urgent' for the second. By the side, the top row is 'important' and the bottom row is 'not important.'

Your top left quadrant is both important and urgent. This is where you need to focus right now. It's going to have a big impact and it's got to be done fast. The top right quadrant is important, but it isn't urgent, so you have the luxury of scheduling it. So that's all the really important stuff either being done or scheduled.

Now you can look at the bottom row, which is not important; that is, it's not mission-critical. Stuff that's urgent, but not important, can safely be delegated or outsourced. As for the box that's neither urgent nor important, you can just take everything in that box off your to-do list, for good. It doesn't need to be done at all.

	URGENT	**NOT URGENT**
IMPORTANT	**DO** Tasks with clear deadlines and significant consequences if not completed in a timely fashion.	**SCHEDULE** Tasks with no set deadline but that bring you closer to your long term goals.
NOT IMPORTANT	**DELEGATE** Tasks that need to get done, but don't need your expertise in order to be completed.	**DELETE** Tasks that distract you from your preferred course, and don't add any measurable value.

I find the Eisenhower matrix a really good way of making clear in my mind what I need to focus on right now. It cuts through the busy-ness and competing calls for attention like a knife through butter. After I have determined what needs to go on my to-do list, I make the list and I will repeat this every day as new work is coming in all of the time. The matrix therefore needs to be flexible to new demands on your time.

Watch out for time-wasters

We are sometimes our own worst enemies when it comes to time management. We waste our own time if we're not aware of our bad habits. Those might be bad personal habits, but equally, an organization can have time-wasting habits built into its culture – an aspect that you'll need to challenge and change.

Do you recognize any of these behaviors in yourself or your organization?

- Worrying and worrying and worrying about something but not taking the decision you need to take?

- Making unrealistic time estimates, so you end up without enough time to do the job properly, or with time slippage all the way through your project?

- Failing to delegate effectively.

- Meetings that are ineffective, don't have clear reasons for the meeting and don't result in clear action plans. Meetings that are just talk, talk, talk.

- Not doing the analysis properly before implementing. Not running a pilot implementation before you go full scale.

- Micro-management.

- Not having good contingency plans. Not having a plan at all!

- Letting work get interrupted all the time by things that may not be important. If people have work packages to get on with, they ought not to be called on suddenly to do something else. Too much interruption comes from poor planning and management.

- Doing what's urgent but not getting round to the really important things that aren't urgent. Fire-fighting and crisis management aren't the way to run things, unless there really *is* a crisis.

- Procrastination.

- Not having standard policies and procedures for things that happen frequently. For instance, if you had to have a full board meeting to decide the price of each item in a retail business, you'd never get work done; if you have an across-the-board policy that says you sell at between two and three times what the item cost, your pricing manager can get on with their job and use their discretion for the exact mark-up for each item.

Strategies to avoid time-wasting

So how can you avoid this kind of time-wasting? First of all, you need to insist on having procedures in place within the organization that stop interrupting work to check up on things. You might want to set up a wiki for your team, as well, or an FAQ, so that all members of the team can quickly check it for basic information. Then you need to plan properly, so that everyone knows what they're meant to be doing, and who needs them to do it – for instance, perhaps your accountant needs to have the monthly results ready for you the day before the divisional meeting.

Plans should come with deadlines. Journalists are used to this: if a paper has to go to print at 11pm, they've got to have the story ready for it! To get the story, the journalist might be on the streets interviewing people, trying to track down a fraudster, phoning from the office, sitting in a magistrate's court taking notes on a case, or doing research in a library. It doesn't matter how they're doing it, but they will have the story ready on time!

Meetings should have a clear reason as well as a clear agenda. Give them a time limit. Take things 'offline' if they don't involve everyone in the meeting, such as if someone has a query about one line of the budget for their particular element of the project. Get things like the minutes of the last meeting agreed in advance so they don't take time up in the meeting. If people are really bad at keeping to time limits, you might organize a standing meeting. When people don't have a chair to sit in, they tend to stay more alert and they're motivated to finish the meeting more quickly. Remember to create clear action points, with deadlines.

Use checklists and to-do lists. You might look at the Japanese *Kanban* management technique (I've included a couple of good books in the bibliography).

Personally, you can avoid time-wasting by concentrating on doing one thing at a time. If you're writing a report, don't answer your emails or start looking through other papers till you've finished. Women are always supposed to be really good at multitasking, but that can be a trap – you need to be able to focus.

Delegate properly, empowering your staff. Micro-management is a waste of your time as well as theirs (when you've built your team properly, you'll be able to trust everyone to do their work without you badgering them).

Break up large projects or tasks into smaller steps that you can get done in one go. Use a day planning calendar or app to organize your day into chunks. If you have a morning routine or a close-of-play routine, that can help. I organize my emails every evening so that I can get started right away the next day and check my planner before I leave the office. And I do the same again in the morning to organize the emails that have come in overnight.

Starting and finishing are often difficult. Take a deep breath and get started; don't sit looking at a job and wondering how you will get it done. Some managers refer to this as JFDI – just f***** do it! As an example, if I have to write a report, sometimes I'll start by just putting down the headings, then filling them in; if I can't think of the right first sentence, I'll do the introduction later. And when you're doing something, make sure you finish it. Hard disks all around the world are full of Chapter Ones from unfinished novels!

Make sure your staff know that they should come to you *before* they get frazzled. If they know they need extra resources to get something done in time, it's better to hear that up front than two days before the deadline when they're tearing their hair out. Ask them to discuss things with you that are important, not just urgent.

Try to show the behavior you'd like your staff to exercise. Don't interrupt them when they're doing an important task. Handle correspondence and queries quickly and concisely. Don't waste other people's time. Be ruthless about saying 'no' to activity that doesn't help you or your team achieve your objectives, and about throwing away things you don't need any more, or at least archiving them (if you need to keep records for regulatory reasons).

If you don't have enough time to do everything, you may need a rethink.

Try to have a set of possible solutions drafted out; you might be able to automate some processes, you might need an extra person on the team, or to relinquish responsibility for a particular process.

Track your time every so often by doing a 'time audit' and encourage team members to do the same (they can keep the results to themselves if they like; you're trying to encourage them to be conscious of how they spend their time, not to 'crack down on timewasting'). Using the Pomodoro technique can also help you work productively: set a timer for twenty-five minutes to work in a focused way on a single thing. Once the timer pings, you can take a break.

And remember that all this time management should give you the room to schedule some time for reflection. Having that time to think about and learn from the day's activity is important. You'll also be able to schedule a little team-togetherness time, a little relaxation, if you all manage to get your tasks done effectively and don't get swamped by firefighting activities.

Time management and priorities

Time management strategies

All these keys to good time management are not going to work unless you understand your priorities. Without this, you won't know what needs to be done first, or what can be left till another day. The Eisenhower matrix should really have helped you with this, as should a clear vision. If your vision is to have the best customer service in the world, then customer problems have to be sorted out before you can start anything else, and the *next* job on the list should be improving your customer service or improving your product quality.

Set yourself up to three priorities every day. More than this and you've got a list that would be nice to do but isn't going to get done. If you're always working on someone else's priorities, you need to make a change. If you are disrupted by 'incoming' distractions then you need to do something about it.

You may find that none of the people making demands on your time actually see the whole of your job. Group finance wants a whole load of statistics provided, but don't see that you have to manage your team and your project as well. Being clear about the way you organize your own time can help you explain to others that you are a limited resource. Remember that leadership is something which in itself takes time, so you will need to make time for coaching and motivating your team, things which may not be visible to others in the organization.

Can you make a case for more resources? If all the tasks you're being loaded with are high priority, then you definitely should.

You may also want to consider a few ways to adjust your working style to cope:

- Work offline when you have a high-priority task (or when you're using the 'Pomodoro' technique).

- Ask customers and managers to create calendar bookings rather than just phoning off the cuff.

- Create a routine for getting certain things done. Mindless routine doesn't help, but having habits that suit you and ensure basic tasks like planning the day and answering emails get done certainly will. My boss structures part of the morning with 10:30-11 talking to team members over coffee, then 11-11:30 'thinking time' which no one is allowed to interrupt.

- Get a day planner. There are plenty of different ones on the market, so do a bit of research first to find the type that will work best for you. You might ask your peers or mentors what works for them.

- Do you have a PA or access to a similar, shared resource? If you are running around phoning people to get them to come to meetings, or on Booking.com trying to book a hotel for next week's management conference, your time could be more constructively used. A PA is not a luxury and delegating tasks like these doesn't make you lazy (besides, if you have someone booking all your team's travel, they'll probably find out how to get you better prices).

- If you're simply under pressure due to a backlog, then get your team to concentrate on clearing the backlog for a while. However, this isn't a long-term option, and if the backlog has been allowed to accumulate for months, you'll need extra resources to do it.

- Don't say "yes" to everything: this causes us to live according to the priorities of others, rather than according to our own. Every time you agree to do something else, something else will not get done. Learn how to say "no."

TIME MANAGEMENT STRATEGIES

- Set up an FAQ to employees can check for basic information
- All meetings should have a clear reason and agenda
- Use checklists and to-do-lists
- Concentrate on one thing at a time
- Delegate
- Break up larger projects into smaller steps
- Use a day planning calendar or app to organize your day
- Be ruthless about saying "no"
- Use the Pomodoro method to set focused time in your day
- Set just three priorities for the day
- Make sure people know you are a limited resource
- Make a case for more resources if needed
- Work offline when working on high priority tasks
- Ask customers and staff to put time in your diary rather than calling spontaneously

- Create routine and habits
- Get a day planner
- Get a PA if needed

Create time for your team

This is something a lot of new leaders have real difficulty with. If you were previously doing a task-orientated job, and now you're leading a team, you'll probably be used to thinking about simply getting your own tasks done. Now, you need to think about the time you need to run your team. You'll need time to help communicate the vision, mission, and the day-to-day priorities. You'll need time to celebrate successes and reward members of the team for their hard work, and you'll need time to help those who are struggling a bit with tough decisions or with new roles or technology.

In fact, as a leader, time spent on your team should be the majority of your time – not 10%, or 20%, but 50 or 60%. If you spend all your time with your head in a spreadsheet, or talking to customers, you're not a leader. So, when you're creating blocks of work in your diary, you want to see lots of entries like these:

- Help John understand the new processes for administering client accounts – thirty minutes.

- Get the team together and praise their work on implementing the new Kanban board – ten minutes (before lunch or at coffee break).

- Talk to Aaliyah about her training course and what she learned (can she present on it to the team later on?) – fifteen minutes.

Remember to hold one-on-ones with team members, not just team meetings. And remember to have enough slack space to listen to what team members really care about – what they did with family at the weekend, a show they saw, a new project they've been thinking about. Studies have shown that women are better listeners and men are better risk takers – use this to your advantage when creating time to listen to your team.

Build in 'thinking time' – time for reflection and introspection. That can be time for your team to talk about what's going well and what's not going so well, how they work as a team, difficulties they have encountered, and potential ways forward. Give your team members the time to think about the development of the team and their own development as individuals.

This might sound like a luxury, but it can produce some really significant business results. For instance, someone who had been behind with their work for a while told me: "It would put my work further behind, but I really think I need help with time management." In the end, she was freed up to take a time management course by reallocating her work across the team – explaining why that needed to be done – and it's improved her contribution and made the team work much more smoothly, since no one has to wait a long time for her to complete tasks anymore.

The more you develop your team and team members, the more you'll be able to delegate, and the better you'll be able to manage your own time. You'll be moving along the curve from 'dealing with what today throws at us' to 'moving forwards and achieving real results,' from firefighting to creating the future.

Step Seven
LEARN THE POWER OF NEGOTIATION

Negotiation is an absolutely basic business skill and even more so for leaders or aspiring leaders. But in a world of supermarkets, where everything comes with a price ticket, we don't learn to bargain as part of daily life. No wonder 40% of Americans say they're not confident in their negotiation skills. A quarter of US employees say they've never negotiated at all.

Yet you really can't get anywhere without being able to negotiate. While skilled negotiators do exist to whom some tasks can be delegated – for instance, negotiations between management and unions – negotiation will be a key part of your role as you move up the career ladder and into a leadership role. Good negotiation skills open up the possibility for all parties to come out on top.

As females, many of us were brought up to share and not to ask for things but to wait until it was offered or given to us. As adults, we can therefore feel uncomfortable asking for things we want or deserve. Women may therefore find it more difficult to negotiate than men do. And this can result in women losing out on promotion or fair salaries.

Early on in your career, you may need to negotiate a raise or a promotion. As a leader, you may need to negotiate:

- A real estate transaction.
- Acquisition of another company.
- The acquisition of your own business by another company.
- A commission split with an affiliate.
- A bulk sales discount with a customer.
- The price of supplies.
- The benefits package for a new employee.

But you may also be negotiating without realizing that this is what you're doing. Many workplace interactions are in fact negotiations. For instance, you might need to negotiate with a team member when you're asking them to do something outside their normal role, such as a special project. You may need to offer them recognition, a bonus, or the chance of promotion, or you may need to ensure that aspects of their normal role are covered by another staff member while they're working on the project. Talking about these issues is, in fact, a negotiation, even if neither of you treat it explicitly as one. So, whether you're a supervisor, or managing a project team, or setting up your own business – even if you're a CEO – you need to be able to negotiate both inside and outside the business.

In fact, you could also look at negotiation as advocacy. It's about articulation and persuasion. For instance, if you want to head up a particular team or department, you need to persuade the other leaders that you're the right person. For someone who wants a promotion, they might start by asking what they'd need to get it, finding out if there are areas they need to brush up on or performance targets to meet; but by doing so, they are setting a marker that they are interested in a promotion. Later, if they meet those targets, they can be more assertive.

As a leader, you may need to be prepared to manage conflict within your team. You'll need to arbitrate, but you may also need to negotiate a solution and to back it up with facts and figures. You may need to be able to suggest a number of alternative solutions and let the team members decide what works best for them.

In fact, some experts reckon that leaders spend up to 80% of their time negotiating. An ability to negotiate well can give you the likelihood of winning better outcomes, something which will enable you and your team to perform better. You'll end up with better relationships than the kind of boss who tries to bludgeon their way into getting what they want. And your team members will be far happier with your leadership if they all feel winners, rather than there being definite winners and losers in the team.

Add to that the fact that if you've negotiated well, and listened to what everyone has to say, you'll probably have ended up with the best possible distribution of resources.

How women can use negotiating skills to their advantage

Prepare!

One thing that women are good at is preparing methodically. Maybe we get that from cutting sandwiches for a picnic with mom and grandma from the time we're three or four. So, use that strength to back up your negotiations.

Prepare by thinking about what you want to achieve and about what you have to offer. Think about the overall context of the negotiation. Is your employer growing fast, or facing new competition and a tough market? What is the market for your particular skills right now? Find out as much as you can about the details of the situation and help by backing up your points with facts.

According to research, women negotiate much more successfully on behalf of others than they do on their own behalf. Women are also less likely to know or to be comfortable expressing their value in dollars than men are. If you want a raise, preparation can really help here. Use Linked In and other resources to find out the normal pay range for your role and level of responsibility. Look at the qualifications most people at your level possess and note if you are more or less qualified. Get evidence for your track record, whether that's accounting statistics, meeting project guidelines, or publications. Try to put yourself in the other party's shoes; what can you offer them and how will they and the organization benefit if you get the role? Consider your counterarguments and think about an effective response. Because this will happen!

Also, think about your company's major objectives. If cost-cutting is one, you'll have a tougher time unless you can point to your ability to put your skills to work to achieve lower costs (perhaps through better purchasing or by improving work processes). If updating the IT system and keeping talent on board are key goals, then you are obviously in a better position.

What's your BATNA? It's your 'best alternative to a negotiated agreement,' that is, it's what you do if negotiations fail. In a supplier negotiation, your BATNA might be the price another supplier has already offered. If you're selling your business, your BATNA might be to keep the business for another five years and grow it, in the hope of a better price once it's got a longer track record. Knowing your BATNA is absolutely crucial to good negotiations and can give you confidence that you know exactly when and where to stop.

The importance of good preparation and intelligence gathering can be shown by the way a friend of mine bought her house. It was a good property, but full of old furniture and papers – not quite a hoarder's lair but not far off. She couldn't quite match the asking price, but she found that due to health issues, the seller needed to move fast to sell, so he could move in with his children. She volunteered to take the house 'as seen', including all the furniture, if she could get a discount. If she hadn't found out that information, she wouldn't have tried to negotiate. As it was, she asked for 10% less than the asking price and ended up with a good deal and a few weekends spent taking stuff to thrift stores.

Think about negotiation as collaboration

Women are used to collaboration, and it can be useful to think about negotiation as a collaboration rather than a competition or confrontation. If you negotiate without considering the other party's needs, you are less likely to achieve a good result. For instance, you may 'win' but at the cost of making enemies or leaving certain parties feeling disgruntled or demotivated. There is no need to be pushy or argumentative; bringing your whole self to the table and connecting on a human level is a much more valuable tactic.

So, one of the things you'll want to do as part of your preparation is to think of the other party's needs and how you can ensure both of you get something you need out of the negotiation. During the negotiation, be willing to seek mutually beneficial solutions and to think creatively.

This style of negotiation is often called 'integrative,' rather than 'distributive' negotiation. Instead of thinking of the other party as an adversary and determining 'gain' and 'loss' by who gets the biggest share of the pie, you're trying to arrive at a solution that will suit both parties.

Use positive emotions and think outside the box

Use positive emotions throughout. Remember if you're asking for a raise that this isn't the only chance you'll get. Even if you don't get a raise now, you've put down a marker. Maybe there's a reason the budget isn't available, but when it is, you'll be rewarded. Maybe you'll be offered an interesting assignment to head up a new team instead. Don't think in terms of win or lose; think in terms of different potential outcomes.

Think of negotiation not as yes or no but an engagement of give and take. Women tend to be good at this. You might be able to give information, an exchange of resources, or a commitment. Look to expand the value of a negotiation by bringing more aspects into it. For instance, if you are trying to buy a company and you have a limit on the cash you can use, as you don't want to increase your business debt, you may not be able to offer the cash price that management wants. Think about other things you could offer. Could you give management shares in the ongoing business? A five-year contract with the enlarged business? A loan note that can be redeemed in three years' time? Being creative is a great advantage when you're negotiating, as many people have fixed objectives and aren't able to keep coming up with alternatives.

Emotional intelligence

Keep listening for more information from the other party throughout the negotiations. What do they want, need, or feel comfortable with? What really bugs them? Many women are good at mining information from people as well as anticipating reactions, so if you have this kind of emotional intelligence, use it. Even if they say things you don't want to hear, information puts you in a better position to advocate for yourself and focus on meeting everyone's needs.

Don't be afraid of silence. Often, leaving a space in the conversation will lead to the other party offering opinions or information that can help you construct a better outcome. Be aware of your own emotions in order to quieten down noisy worries or fears, but also be aware of the other party's emotions. Are there particular suggestions that make them bristle? Are they looking interested, bored, angry, or thoughtful? Don't be afraid to hear the word "no." It isn't something to fear; you won't be any worse off than you were before you started, always remember that.

Be calm. If you are in charge of the timing of the meeting, then for instance, if someone else got promoted instead of you, wait till your aggrieved feelings die down. You need to be able to ask calmly and in a neutral voice what you could have done better, or whether you lacked particular skills or qualifications. You won't get the promotion, but you probably *will* get useful information which you can use to address any shortcomings and make a future promotion more likely.

(On the other hand, if you run straight into your boss' office and yell: "Why didn't I get that promotion? I deserved it!" you have probably said goodbye to your career progression with that organization).

Other negotiating tips

Keep evolving new scenarios and be flexible

You should already have gone into negotiations with a plan for different reactions and counter-offers, and what you would do in each case. But as you learn more about the other party's motivations and needs, you should keep evolving new scenarios. Be flexible if the other party suggests something you haven't thought of.

If rather than just negotiating for an increase in salary, you also volunteer to take on additional responsibilities or achieve a different performance target. You'll be more positively perceived by showing yourself as giving something, being flexible, not just taking.

I always like to remember the story of how one manager went into a meeting determined to negotiate for a raise. Instead, she was offered a chance to buy her part of the business in a management buy-out. She asked for time-out to consider her option – you can always ask for time if new information becomes available – and in the end, secured a bank loan enabling her to become CEO of the new business. It was not quite what she'd asked for... but definitely a win for her. If she had not gone in with an open mind, she may never have ended up in that position.

Practice makes perfect

It takes practice to be a great negotiator. Why not start negotiating by practicing at a flea market or antiques fair, where your emotions and self-worth aren't involved? For instance, just asking "Is that your best price?" is a good start; you could also ask if you can get a better price if you buy more than one piece, or, if you're buying a large piece and the owner doesn't want to discount, if they could add in a small thing you have your eye on for the same price. Remember to keep a record of how much you've saved! This can really build your confidence for when you need to negotiate at work.

You might also prepare by 'wargaming' with a friend or mentor or role-playing a negotiation with them. And listen to how other experienced negotiators do it; you could learn a lot!

Negotiate for others, not just yourself!

Negotiating hard for their own interests can sometimes put women at risk of being regarded as bossy or aggressive. Ensuring a win/win result can help avoid this, as can negotiating on behalf of a group or on behalf of other people in your organization. If you're trying to get resources, frame the negotiation as ensuring your team members have adequate support, rather than as you arguing for your own little fiefdom. You'll want to talk about 'we need' – the needs of your team – rather than saying 'I want,' in order to position yourself this way.

Don't make assumptions

Often, parties to a negotiation assume that they know exactly what the other party wants. This can lead to a fairly hostile atmosphere if you assume that you are on the opposite side from the other party and they must want exactly the opposite of what you want.

Find out the other party's motivations and try to think through the negotiation from their point of view. What kind of concessions might help achieve the result you want? What is their most important objective and how can you help them achieve it? For instance, a supplier might offer a significantly better price in return for a five-year contract, if they have another customer who is threatening to switch and they want security.

Ensure that neither you nor the other party have preconceived ideas about each other and each other's motivations; don't make implicit assumptions. This is why information is so important.

NEGOTIATING SKILLS

- Prepare
- Consider your BATNA
- Collaborate rather than confront
- Use positive emotions
- Think outside the box
- Give and take
- Get into listening mode

- Don't be afraid of silence or of hearing the word "no"
- Be calm
- Keep evolving new scenarios
- Be flexible
- Practice makes perfect
- Negotiate for others, not just yourself
- Don't make assumptions of the other party's wants and needs
- Prepare for the questions you might be asked

Step Eight

DEVELOP A HIGH-
PERFORMANCE TEAM

A s a leader, putting together a high performing team is one of the most important things you will do, and is an essential skill you will need to acquire.

The first step in developing a high-performance team is to surround yourself with great people. You might hire them, you might be lucky enough to find them, or you may have to transform your people into great people – or rather, help them transform themselves from 'frog' to 'prince.'

Getting great people isn't easy without good leadership. Covid lockdowns made many people rethink what their lives were really about, and that led to the 'Great Resignation' as some fled jobs that were no longer what they really wanted to do. Enterprises now have to offer more flexible working, as well as good salaries, to attract talent. But people also want to work somewhere they are appreciated, and to get really high performance, you need to make them feel highly valued, confident, and motivated.

What is a high-performing team? In short, it is a team of goal-focused individuals who align to the same goals, with complementary skills to achieve superior results.

Often, managers build teams that are homogenous, so everyone has the same kind of personality, the same skillset, or the same way of working. But that doesn't necessarily achieve high performance. Your team could be very diverse: it might have some members who are finance rocket scientists, some who have relatively little experience, a few way-out, creative types, some people who work solo and others who are very collaborative and there to facilitate life for other team members. In fact, a diverse team might perform much better than a more homogenous team.

So, what is it that creates high performance?

First of all, high performance relies on having a common goal which every member of the team understands and commits to. They should also understand how their own work feeds into achieving that goal. For instance, a football team might include a medic or health scientist. It's not going to be her job to score a goal, but she knows that if she can keep the footballers in top form, they're more likely to win their games. It's also about a shared vision. Again, taking an example from the world of football, Juergen Klopp, at Liverpool, has a very clear vision of what his club represents and where he wants it to go.

Klopp also understands the importance of emotion in team achievement. He's very highly regarded as a motivator, because he creates a relationship of mutual respect with his players. That's another key to high performance: if you don't trust your employees, or they don't trust you, it will be much more difficult to perform. And Klopp's touchline celebrations when his team scores a goal are well known – check out 'Jurgen Klopp crazy goal celebrations' on YouTube if you haven't seen him react! Celebrating successes is another key to high performance, because it gets the team in the habit of winning, together.

On the subject of success and emotion, positive psychology research has shown the powerful benefits that happiness can bring. Sean Achor, a professor at Harvard has studied happiness in the workplace and how it can impact the success and performance of a team. In his book, 'The

Happiness Advantage,' he shares his latest discoveries on this. In one large company that he looked at, he realized that managers who felt the most pressure from their jobs, had the lowest net profits and performance. He discovered that even a small burst of happiness had an immediate impact on the performance of those teams. Check out his book if you haven't already – he talks about some really interesting stuff. This highlights the importance of having a happy team to ensure peak performance. The things we will talk about in this chapter will go a long way towards achieving this.

As well as having a happy team, a high-performing team is also about good communication. It's about clarity, with defined roles and responsibilities, and work managed on the basis of priorities with appropriate deadlines. A team won't perform well unless it has the right structures to support it, from budget spreadsheets to morning meetings, monthly reports or milestone reporting on projects.

Finally, the top performing teams are always notable for one very important factor: they are committed to continuous learning and improvement. They will keep developing, and the individuals within the team will also improve their skills.

What to think about when you're building your team

Team qualities

The first thing to consider when you're building a team is its optimal size. A lot of studies have been carried out on how big a team should be, and the consensus is that you probably shouldn't go much over eight or nine people without breaking it down into sub-teams. If you think of the interconnections between people, they increase exponentially with the size of the team. Two people only have one connection; three people have three (A talks to B, B to C and C to A); four people have six (A talks to B, B to C, C to D, B to D, A to C, and A to D) and by the time you get to seven people, you have twenty-one different relationships. Once you get to ten, it's impossible for any individual in the team to keep count.

On the other hand, if you only have two or three people in a team, you may not have enough diversity of skills, and personality issues can have a negative impact, as you don't have enough people to cool down a disagreement between two people.

That suggests teams are best around five to eight people – not much fewer, and not many more. In my team, for each client relationship we have, we typically have five of us working on that team, which seems to work well; teams also contain a mix of junior and senior staff.

Secondly, think about diversity. You need different skills and different personalities. Belbin's Nine Team Roles are a good way to think about personalities: some people are good at detail, some better at the big picture; some are creative, others methodical or analytical. Using the Nine Team Roles should help you ensure you get a good mix of types. Let's take a look at them now.

Belbin's Nine Team Roles	
Resource investigator	Inquisitive, finds ideas to bring to the team
Teamworker	Facilitator, helps the team to communicate and collaborate
Co-ordinator	Clarifies goals, allocates work, delegates
Plant	Highly creative problem-solver
Monitor evaluator	Weighs up the evidence, highly analytical
Specialist	Brings in-depth knowledge
Shaper	Provides drive, energy

Belbin's Nine Team Roles	
Implementer	Turns ideas into actions, makes things work
Completer finisher	Detail-orientated, perfectionist, ties up loose ends

You should also think about diversity in terms of the mix of gender, nationalities, backgrounds, experience, and age. A team that is completely made up of middle-aged graduates with accountancy qualifications is going to be short on marketing skills, and it won't have 'digital native' millennials who understand the new generation of smartphone banking and payment systems. In my organization, we try to find people with a diversity of skills on our teams, so we have a broad skillset and are ready for whatever challenges the future brings.

Talk to prospective team members about their life experiences and about their plans for the future. Try to get a good proportion of members with good EQ (emotional intelligence) who can interact with others and help facilitate within the team. Find team members who want to learn; they may say they want to get experience of a particular type of project or a particular subject area, for instance. And when you're choosing, think about getting the right mix, not just getting the right person for a job. It's like casting a play: a casting director has to try to get some electricity between the lead roles in a love story, and to get actors different enough in looks, voice and energy that the play comes alive.

Team structure and goals

Once you have put your team together, you haven't finished. You've made the team, but now you have to breathe life into it, and you have to give it structure and purpose. First, you need to create a clear mission and a shared sense of purpose. Get people not just committed to that purpose but enthusiastic about it, and you'll start off with good energy. Make sure the team share the same values. For instance, in a band, if you have three musicians who believe they need to produce a totally consistent sound and interpretation, and a fourth who believes in a more improvisational way of making music, there's always going to be tension.

Next, you'll want to create clear, common and measurable goals; otherwise, you won't achieve much. Take a bird's eye approach to ensure each person is given the right roles and responsibilities; each person should know how they fit into the goal.

You will need to ensure that work isn't being duplicated; there is nothing more demotivating than finishing a task and realizing someone else has beat you to it! Clearly defining roles and responsibilities will ensure that this doesn't happen.

Create project milestones that you can track, for the team as a whole and for individual team members. Think about how often you need to track progress; that will depend on a number of things including the purpose of the team, how often you need to report up the line, and how long you expect a project to last. This will ensure that people are kept on track and also helps with communication within the team if they can provide regular updates on where they're up to.

Inspire your team

It is vital that your team feel inspired; people work best when they have a purpose and can connect on an emotional level. Ensure that each individual in your team feels connected to the goals, taking into account their personal or overall goals. How can they grow? What will engage them emotionally and intellectually?

Regular one-to-one meetings can help here as it allows them to talk about their career aspirations and performance goals.

Think about the different ways your team can collaborate. This is particularly important if your team work remotely most of the time. Since the pandemic, many organizations have started to set up more collaboration areas within the office to encourage teams to get away from their desks and discuss ideas.

Processes need to be made as seamless as possible. How can you do this? Are there any time-wasting actions that can be eliminated?

Set up formal lines of communication

Of course, you'll also be encouraging your team members to communicate and collaborate with each other. Openness is important to allow teams to function at high performance levels, and you'll want to ask team members for feedback on how you can help them become productive. When you're putting work processes in place, ask the team what they prefer – virtual meetings, face to face, on-site or away from the office. Some may prefer to log into a task management system every day, while others may want to be able to take a few days to get work done and bring it back into the team when they are satisfied with it. Make sure team members understand the system is just there as a support structure, and that they are free to share ideas, tasks or information freely in the team.

Opening up the lines of communication also makes it easier to spot minor problems that may have later led to more significant problems had they not been caught early. Keeping team members informed of what others are doing through regular meetings or other forms of communication means team members understand each other's role and what stage of a project they're at and gives an opportunity to ask questions or for help. We have bi-weekly meetings in my team, which are a chance to really open up, ask questions and share ideas.

For any big pieces of news our leadership want to share, we hold regular town halls – these are a great way to get everyone together and gives people an opportunity to ask questions about any changes that are being made in the organization.

Learn how to listen actively and how to ask questions. A leader who facilitates a team meeting so everyone can contribute is far more effective than a leader who talks all the time. And above all, make sure all your team members feel that they are valued.

Build trust

Make it clear that people can come to you with anything they need; this helps build trust and helps the team see you as approachable. This is a crucial part of leadership. Your team depend on you and need to be able to trust you and approach you with absolutely anything on their mind.

Without trust, you do not have a high-performing team.

Support them to reach their goals, but also give them some breathing space so that they can forge their own paths. Allow them to do what they do best; research has shown that this is when we are happiest.

Be genuine. If it's your first team and you're anxious about taking on responsibility, don't fake a confidence you don't feel; be honest with the team that it's your first time as a team leader, so this will be a learning experience for you as well as for the team. Don't shirk the tough conversations or decisions. If there's a major problem or if one team member isn't pulling their weight, be honest and be fair.

Continual development

Make your team a learning team that is committed to continual development. For instance, share feedback with each other regularly; if team members haven't engaged in constructive feedback before, show them how to use it to achieve improvement. Have a personal development plan for every member of the team and ask team members who have learned new skills or work methods to share them so the team as a whole can learn.

Resolve conflict

Open communication can prevent many conflicts you may face, which means it can be addressed early on. Never let conflicts foster, as they can spread through the team like wildfire. Remind people that you're all on the same side, working as a team, so there is no need to compete. I remember in a previous job, there were certain individuals who thought it would further their careers if they were competitive with their colleagues. All this did was foster a culture of distrust and suspicion. It was not a pleasant environment to work in. Leadership could have nipped it in the bud, but it was left to grow until it was so bad that I had to leave.

A high-performing team can be a huge asset to the enterprise. You'll have employees who are motivated and enthusiastic; you'll be able to improve the service you can offer to clients; and your team members will be able to work independently and bring new knowledge and skills into the organization.

Motivating your team

Management theory abounds in theories about what motivates people. The truth, though, is that we're all different; what motivates one person may not motivate another. Sometimes, people will have different motivations at different points in their careers. But whatever it is that motivates them, the fact is that motivated team members are 50% more likely to exceed their performance targets, according to Hay Group research.

As with confidence, so with motivation, men and women often tend to have rather different outlooks. Women tend to depend on regular recognition and appreciation for motivation, which is understandable when you think of what we found out about women's relative lack of confidence.

Don't make assumptions, though. While many women are moms and will be thrilled to get the chance to strike a better work-life balance, for instance by working at home two days a week, some women may be more motivated by the chance to travel. Women may also be motivated by the chance to work in a team and by working for a boss who shows empathy.

Men tend to be more motivated by competitiveness and being the best at what they do, as well as by the desire to meet deadlines and to be more goal-orientated. However, some men may be carers for an unwell parent or partner, while others may be more driven by the desire to serve others. The best way to motivate people is to know them well personally and understand their circumstances and what they want to get out of life.

Motivational expert James Sale divides employees into nine types, each of whom can be motivated in a different way. Often, people combine two or three of the different types. The table below shows the types, what they value, and how you can use that to motivate them.

Type	What they value	What motivates them
Defender	Security, stability	Keep them in the loop, give them clear goals and explicit feedback, reward them for loyalty
Friend	Belonging, friendship, empathy	Create a good team feeling, discuss work issues with them, ensure they feel valued
Star	Recognition, respect	Give them awards or status, involve them in projects, give them learning opportunities and opportunities to shine, and reward them very visibly
Director	Power, influence, control	Motivate them by giving them more responsibility, opportunities to depulise, secondments, training, coaching. Stretch them to their limits
Builder	Material possessions, money	Give them financial rewards clearly linked to performance, as well as progression opportunities. Engage their competitive spirit
Expert	Knowledge, skill	Give them training and learning opportunities, opportunities to be seen as 'the expert,' or to mentor others

Type	What they value	What motivates them
Creator	Innovation, creativity, change	Reward them for innovation; don't put them in routine roles. Give them interesting and challenging side projects
Spirit	Autonomy and freedom	Can be motivated by sharing the vision, then delegate responsibility to them and let them do their thing. Easily demotivated by too much procedure
Searcher	Wants to make a difference	Give them a purpose, help them see the bigger picture, reward them for their input to the team as a whole

Often, people prefer the flexibility to make their own choice of package. For instance, offering salary sacrifice schemes, whereby employees can choose a lower salary in exchange for a better car, higher pension contributions, or more days holiday, lets employees choose for themselves what is most important to them.

My organization has become even more flexible in where its employees can work since the pandemic. Hybrid working is now a formal way of working that we have adopted and feedback has shown that this is one of the major motivators for many of our employees. The research also showed that people value more time with their family, more so now than ever before. So, the option to buy additional holidays is a welcome benefit. As a leader, is there anything you would be able to offer your employees to help motivate them? Examples may include free lunches, private medical insurance or special leave for time off when they have personal issues to deal with.

Remember that the general atmosphere of the team itself will also affect motivation. If you've established a positive attitude, with open communications and no talking about people behind their backs, and you give good, constructive feedback to the team members, they are likely to be well motivated. If they share the overall vision and are given achievable but demanding goals, they'll want to do well.

Giving team members the chance to mentor or to be mentored, to learn through training courses (on or offsite, or online), and to contribute to decision-making, will also help motivate them.

Five things high-performing teams do differently

A report in Harvard Business Review looked at the main differences in behavior between high-performing teams and also-rans (the opposite of a high performing team). High performance is gained by fulfilling members' needs for autonomy (freedom), competence (skills, training), and relatedness (communication, empathy, team spirit). The third is the most difficult to fulfill; staff may not particularly like each other outside the team environment, or want to be personal friends, but they need to feel some kind of kindred spirit.

Covid has made things even more difficult now that team members may not see each other face-to-face on a regular basis. While working from home has been a boon for autonomy, empowering many to decide when and where they work, a lack of physical proximity to colleagues has made it exponentially more challenging to create close personal bonds.

Yet new research suggests that the highest-performing teams have found subtle ways of leveraging social connections during the pandemic to fuel their success. The findings offer important clues on ways any organization can foster greater connectedness – even within a remote or hybrid work setting – to engineer higher-performing teams.

1. They pick up the phone much more often. Phoning other members of the team is a regular way of catching up and keeping in touch. High levels of communication are maintained between all the

different team members.

2. They plan their meetings more strategically. They don't just have meetings because it's Monday and they always have a Monday meeting. The agenda is structured to be relevant to the most important work streams or issues rather than 'going through the motions.'

3. They invest time bonding over non-work topics. For instance, two team members might take ten minutes to talk about their children's letters to Santa, or about binge-watching The Sopranos. 'Water-cooler talk' brings people together in a genuine way.

4. Everyone delivers mutual appreciation rather than expecting the leader to act like a teacher and give gold stars. Members of the team openly praise others' work.

5. Great teams have emotional authenticity – that is, team members feel it is safe to talk about their feelings with colleagues, whether they're feeling energetic, doubtful, unconfident or enthusiastic.

In other words, a great team is a great place to hang out. It's a place that team members feel valued and appreciated as people, not just workers, and that they feel safe to be honest with other members of the team.

Surrounding yourself with great people

If you are a leader of sheep, you're not really a leader; you're a shepherd. Real leaders don't lead sheep; they lead teams made up of truly great people. And real leaders ensure that whoever joins their team becomes a truly great person.

Steve Jobs famously said: "It doesn't make sense to hire smart people and tell them what to do; we hire smart people so they can tell us what to do." Leadership is not about knowing all the answers; leadership is about being humble enough to listen to the people you've hired. If you can hire people who are smarter than you, do it. It's a decision that will more than repay the investment.

Of course, if you hire people who are smarter than you, then you need to trust them get on with their work without your chasing them. If you don't empower sheep, they just carry on saying "baa"; but if you don't empower smart people, they will either start to behave like sheep, or they'll leave your team and try to find a leader who will appreciate them properly.

Remember that some of your peers are great people, too. Stay in touch with them, use them as a sounding board for ideas, and leverage their expertise if it will benefit your team.

If you look at great leaders, they're surrounded by great people. Queen Elizabeth I was surrounded by great people – men of action like Sir Walter Raleigh and Sir Francis Drake, or men of letters like her spymasters Cecil and Walsingham. Film director Martin Scorsese has built a team of great actors like Leonardo di Caprio, Robert De Niro, Harvey Keitel, and Daniel Day-Lewis, and leads a team of filmmakers including Oscar winners such as editor Thelma Schoonmaker, cinematographer Robert Richardson, and costume designer Sandy Powell. And failed leaders are usually surrounded by yes-men and second-rate followers. Remember, you will be judged on the people you lead, as well as on your leadership.

Company culture

We have not really touched on this in great detail, but I think it is an important consideration when creating a high-performing team. How exactly do you define company culture? In the 1980s, two consultants, Deal and Kennedy, defined it as "The way we do things around here." Others may say it is the way they behave or the mindset they have, but in short, it is a value system that encapsulates an organization's shared values and characteristics.

Once you've been around a company for a while, you can sniff out some of those values and even small things can tell you a lot. Are people wearing suits or casual clothes, or suits but without a tie? Are you the only woman in the room? In particular, culture will determine how people relate to each other and how they respond to change. For instance, the company may structure relations hierarchically, or it may have a relatively flat structure. That will determine how free a junior person feels to speak out or to ask questions. It may be very collaborative, or there may be a culture of promoting 'stars,' which will tend to make people act in a more individualistic way rather than as team members.

Why does it play such a pivotal role in creating a high-performing team? Well, first of all, company culture is a major reason employees stay with the business, so it reduces turnover, which creates high morale. It leads to increased productivity and willingness to meet tough challenges. Some quite interesting research shows that companies with top quartile culture make shareholder returns up to 200% higher than other businesses and that doesn't come from poor-performing teams. If all employees share the culture, collaboration between them will be much easier.

How can you ensure that your company has a great culture which attracts great talent? If you're part of a large organization, you will need to work with the other leaders to create the cultural values. If you're a business owner or leader of a small company, it is more than likely wholly up to you to create the company culture. Think about other places you have worked where you have really valued particular aspects of the culture. Think about why the company exists, what makes it different, what your values are, what customers expect and what kind of employees you need to attract. This will give you a great starting point. Good cultures work to help the company deliver its mission and minimize wastage and employee churn. They might include an absence of petty office politics, high involvement and enthusiasm from staff, and readiness to celebrate wins at all levels. A good culture is likely to be transparent, with clear values and accessible, visible leaders, and a clear mission and values; all these aspects help employees do the right things and promote high performance. For instance, if you don't have clear values, it makes decisions much more difficult since people don't know what to prioritize.

My organization's culture promotes diversity and inclusion and a place where everyone can bring their whole selves to work, encouraging honest and open communication. We care about global warming and helping others less fortunate in society, as well as supporting various charities.

On the other hand, some companies have quite a toxic culture. Sometimes this is deliberate; I knew one company that had way over 100% staff turnover a year, but where top management believed in what they called corporate Darwinism, getting rid of the weakest. The problem was that since employees could see how easy it was to be fired for no good reason, the good ones decided to go elsewhere, and motivation was poor – but the managers still thought they were doing the right thing.

Thinking about and then building a good company culture takes a lot of discipline and time. Give it the time it deserves – and don't leave it till you've answered your emails!

Step Nine
ADAPT FOR EFFECTIVE LEADERSHIP IN A POST-COVID WORLD

What has changed?

As a leader, it is important to address the changes that have taken place in the workplace due to the pandemic and how this may impact your role.

Having to manage businesses when employees were locked up in their homes was one of the biggest challenges most leaders have faced in the last decade. Managers who had resisted teleworking for years were forced to manage a distributed team via phone, email and Zoom or Teams calls. It looks certain that although much is now going back to normal, remote workforces and more distributed workforces will become far more prevalent in future and firms need to adapt to this on a long-term basis.

EY's 'Work Reimagined' survey showed that both employees and employers recognize the need for a hybrid and flexible work policy and some 80% of employees want to work at least two days a week remotely; meanwhile, 72% of employers either have a policy allowing remote work, or are working on one. Nearly three-quarters of employers are willing to hire scarce talent with critical skills from anywhere in the world – and they can work wherever they like. At the extreme, 'digital nomads' travel the world while working from their laptops, usually (though not always) as freelancers.

This isn't new; teleworking has been with us for a long time. But the scale of the phenomenon has changed drastically. So have the specifics. There might be some staff working permanently from home or working two days a week at home and three on site, while others simply request time at home when they are writing a report or doing some other task requiring continuous concentration. Distributed teams may include workers in different locations; offshoring and outsourcing have become common so that some team members may be freelancers or members of another organization.

Younger people in particular expect flexibility of working and are likely to quit if they don't get it. In fact, they may not even apply for a job with a company that's seen as inflexible on this point. Post-Covid, quality of life and work-life balance have become important topics, and 43% of employees surveyed by EY said they were likely to leave their employer in the next twelve months. Among Generation Z and Millennials, this increased to over half, and for those working in IT and hardware, to 60%. Talent can no longer be taken for granted.

The old status quo has disappeared. So, it's important that, as a leader, you take on board the fact that employees can and will switch jobs if they don't get what they want. You need to understand what your team members value, and it's unlikely to be just higher pay or a promotion all of the time.

Most employees prefer a rewards policy including flexible benefits, the possibility of more time off (or a sabbatical), healthcare programs, and even additional support for caregiving (in the case of nearly 10% of employees).

Gen Z wants to stay socially connected while working, values a change of 'job scenery' and cares more about the design of their workplace. And the more an employee cares about such things, the more likely they are to leave if they don't get them.

The great news for women (and men) with children is that rather than one partner being at home all the time, partners can split their work and home responsibilities. Admittedly, since there are five days in a week and not four or six, the split may still have to be unequal!

People also care about the environment, which may have been rapidly progressed by the movement Greta Thunberg has created amongst young people. They want to work for an organization that cares about climate change and is willing to take action to fight it. My organization has a target to be net zero by 2025. All the talk of reduced carbon emissions during the pandemic lockdowns when there were much fewer flights and people weren't traveling for business, has only put this higher up people's agenda and they want to work for companies that put sustainability at the center of their business.

Diversity and inclusion have become much more important topics in the workplace. If you truly want to thrive, D&I should be incorporated into your organization's strategy and be at the heart of your workforce.

You'll likely have heard about Quiet quitting which seems to be spreading worldwide as another way to quit your job. Employees who feel uninspired, underappreciated, or overworked may begin to check out long before they give you their two weeks' notice. But great leaders can have a real impact on retention using the ways we have discussed in this book.

The risks and challenges of remote working for the enterprise

Risks
There are a number of risks to adopting remote working, many of

which arise because the regulatory and legal status of remote workers, particularly those working in another country, is not yet clearly defined.

For instance, employers in most countries are responsible for payroll taxes. However, suppose you employ someone who works from home, and then moves country, where are they resident for tax purposes? (Some of these issues needed to be addressed during the pandemic, when lockdowns prevented those working in another country from getting back home).

There may be regulatory issues. For instance, EU law states that personal data of EU citizens may not be released outside the EU unless they have previously given consent. An EU firm using a digital nomad who was working from Bali or Albania might easily fall foul of these regulations.

Immigration rules may also be an issue. Do they have the right to work in that country if they're working remotely in a different county to where they're employed? An increasing number of countries now offer digital nomad visas but this is something you will need to look into. You'll also want to know where people are at any given time, for instance if you need to get them out of a conflict zone or if there's another pandemic lockdown.

Cybersecurity is a major issue for the distributed enterprise. Data management, authentication, and strong encryption will be needed to prevent communications being intercepted and to ensure only authorized personnel gain access to your organization's systems. There are different rules on what styles of encryption may be used in different countries, so your IT team will need to be on top of these.

And if you have teams which included members from countries with widely varying living costs, you'll need to think about how to handle pay rates. This can be particularly sensitive if you're using digital nomad staff, as home country employees in, say, Indonesia are unlikely to be happy if they find out an American living in Bali is getting several times their pay rate for doing the same job.

Organizations will need to think through these issues and stay on top of ever-changing regulations. You might also think about whether you should allow the organization's response to be driven by employee requirements, or whether you should move to go faster in order to acquire scarce talents or even to reduce corporate costs significantly.

Real estate

A higher proportion of remote employees together with more flexible working for site-based staff is likely to require big changes to the organization's real estate. It could enable some organizations to cut the square footage they rent or own considerably.

But offices are currently structured for the traditional world of on-site working, not for flexible working. You need to do more than a superficial refresh with new desks and a few tins of paint. Start thinking about an integrated workplace that is flexible enough to let teams design their own workspace according to their current needs, and that has amenities to empower workers to become productive. My own employer has reconfigured our workspace to create more collaborative and team working space, so when people come into the office, they're spending their time with the team, not just doing paperwork or logging on to the systems they could use at home.

Eventually, perhaps, offices will reverse the current ratio of desks to meeting rooms, so that there are few or even no individual workspaces.

There are some other interesting opportunities opened up by moving to flexible working. In some businesses, there used to be a huge gap between the mainly mobile 'road warriors' in sales, and office-based employees. Now, that polarization can disappear, and you can integrate mobile salespeople easily into product development teams, for instance. That means you're getting feedback direct from the frontline people who see clients and understand that point of view.

Maybe 'your own desk' and 'the corner office' have lost their appeal.

When you're thinking about real estate, though, it's important to remember employees' needs. Not everyone has plenty of spare space for an office at home. Younger employees who share a home with three or four friends may find it difficult to concentrate in a busy and crowded apartment. During Covid lockdowns, many women (and more than a few men) found it very difficult to combine their work life with school-age children staying at home all day.

You also need to consider whether employees working from home will be caught out by zoning rules, planning permissions, or condominium/leasehold rules that prevent them 'running a business' from residential premises. You'll want an expert who can advise your staff on these issues. You may also want to assist employees setting up their workspace at home, with advice, and maybe financially or with the loan of furnishings and equipment.

IT issues

With workers who, for whatever reason, don't have familiarity with networking, collaborative and social technology, consider training them so they feel confident using it. But you might also want to rethink the look and feel of your systems. Take a look at different small business accounting systems to understand how different the experience of using them can be – Sage looks like a rather cluttered spreadsheet, while Zoho and Wave feel more like social apps with lots of graphs and visual representations.

If you need help envisioning what your workplace applications *could* look like, hire someone from the world of consumer apps. If you've used Uber or Amazon, you can see how to streamline processes; that's the experience you're looking for. Remember, too, that for Gen Z it's the smartphone or tablet, not the desktop, that is their prime device. Building applications that don't allow access through Android or iPhone apps is really a mistake, though if you grew up in the 1980s, you might have difficulty believing it.

Adapting job culture

Old style micro-managers will certainly be out of a job in a distributed organization. You can't see what your staff are doing out of the corner of your eye or pop in on them unannounced. You'll need a job culture that focuses on outcomes and rewards collaboration. Encourage your team to give credit for those who help solve problems or find difficult-to-access information, so you know how well they are working together. If someone from another department has given valuable input to your team, make sure you feed that back to their manager.

Some macho behaviors like being seen to be the earliest to arrive and the last to leave will lose potency once flexible working becomes normal. Something many women will particularly value is that once a two-to-three-day home-office split becomes the norm, home working and part time will no longer be seen as 'mommy track' options. In other words, you'll be able to achieve a good work-life balance without being seen as unambitious or uncommitted.

It's possible that career shapes could change, too. Previously, the idea was that you'd have a linear progression, working your way up each level of the organization. Post-Covid, we might see a move towards careers that are more diffuse and diverse, maybe with workers taking on more challenges in different areas, or joining a number of teams rather than having a single job title. That gives more ways to build in sabbaticals, childcare, part time working, or paternity leave, alongside secondments, 'sandwich' courses or part-time MBAs, and other training needs.

Hire the future

Changes in the world of work are being driven by younger people, so get some Gen Z on the team and ensure their views are listened to. Assuming they will have the same career and life objectives as someone in their fifties is a mistake, as is reading about them as if they are exotic creatures. They're not; they're just humans who happen to be younger, and who can – and should – speak for themselves.

A friend of mine works in a bar, but now she's in her late forties, she's not as good as she was at being able to see the difference between a twenty-one-year-old drinker (perfectly legal) and a seventeen-year-old (definitely not legal). So, she has two secret weapons. One is a twenty-two-year-old, who has almost a 100% record of being able to guess customers' ages to within a few months. The other is a local schoolteacher, who knows just how old *all* the kids in town are, because she taught them.

How to lead in the Great Resignation

The biggest challenge to leadership is how to create a sense of shared vision when people are not only working in different places, but may never have met in real life, and when you need to lead a team composed of both 'internet natives' and people for whom the internet arrived once their careers were already established, and who have quite different outlooks.

Your challenge is to keep up daily communication without micro-managing – checking *in* rather than checking *up*, so to speak. You'll need to offer feedback and appreciation freely, without being asked for it. You'll need to be a problem-solver on behalf of your team, so you are the first person they want to call as a sounding-board or to highlight an issue that might become a roadblock.

You'll need to invest in the people you already have and help them have the life they want while working to achieve your common objectives. You'll need to decide what are the core competencies that you need, and where they need to be deployed. And you'll need to put human beings at the center of your leadership – and make sure they know it. So, let's look at what you've learned in this book, and where you could go next.

Conclusion

I n this book, you've learned about the difference between simply managing, and becoming a leader. We talked about the traits of great leaders, their long-term vision, their ability to communicate it, and their ability to continue to learn, and to help their people develop as well. You've also seen some characteristics which work well for women in leadership – inclusivity, empathy, and valuing work-life balance for themselves and their staff.

You've seen how men and women often communicate in different ways, sometimes leading to misunderstandings. That's something you can address once you understand it: learn to be more assertive, don't apologize so often, don't let men interrupt you when you're speaking.

We looked at different kinds of leadership. That may have resonated with you. Did you feel "Oh, I'm a servant leader!" or maybe "Yes, I probably depend on bureaucratic leadership?" Do you feel more of an autocratic or democratic leader? Wherever you are on the spectrum, you can achieve great things – but you need to understand where you're starting from.

We also talked about confidence and how important it is in leadership. Yet many women have issues with not feeling confident, and even feeling like imposters who will inevitably get found out. Building your confidence is never going to be easy, but setting about it the right way, you'll continually reinforce positive feelings. Dealing with imposter syndrome might be the single thing you need to do to stop struggling, and start leading.

We've just seen a huge change in our lives with two years of Covid lockdowns leading to supply chain disruptions, more remote working, and the 'great resignation,' just at the time we have the second generation of digital natives hitting the workforces. In a time of change, leadership comes to the fore. And it's an exciting prospect – leading the way to a new and more inclusive workplace. So, it's time for you to take up the challenge of leadership, and find out what you can really achieve!

Sources
BOOKS, REPORTS AND ACADEMIC JOURNALS

Babcock, Linda. *Women Don't Ask: Negotiation and the Gender Divide*
Princeton University Press. 2003

Benson, Jim. *Personal Kanban: Mapping Work – Navigating Life*
Modus Cooperandi Press. 2011

Burrows, Mike. *Kanban From The Inside*
Blue Hole Press. 2014.

Cabane, Olivia Fox. *The Charisma Myth: How Anyone Can Master the Art and Science of Personal Magnetism*

Daskal, Lolly. *The Leadership Gap: What Gets Between You and Your Greatness*
Penguin Publishing Group. 2017

Ehrlinger, J. and Dunning, D. *How Chronic Self-Views Influence (and Potentially Mislead) Estimates of Performance*
Journal of Personality and Social Psychology. 2003; 84 (1): 5–17. DOI: <10.1037/0022-3514.84.1.5>

Harris, Russ. *The Confidence Gap: A Guide to Overcoming Fear and*

Self-doubt
Shambala. 2011

Institute for Leadership and Management *Ambition and gender at work:*
ILM Report https://www.institutelm.com/resourceLibrary/ambition-
and-gender-at-work.html; 2011

Jeffers, Susan. *Feel the Fear and Do It Anyway*
Vermilion. 2007

Kouzes, James and Posner, Barry. *The Leadership Challenge*
Wiley. 2007

Kahnweiler, Elizabeth B. *The Introverted Leader: Building on Your Quiet*
Strength
Berrett-Koehler Publishers. 2018

Kolb, Deborah M and Porter, Jessica L. *Negotiating at Work: Turn Small*
Wins into Big Gains
Wiley. 2015

Ross, J. A., Scott, G. and Bruce, C. D. *The Gender Confidence Gap*
in Fractions Knowledge: Gender Differences in Student Belief–
Achievement Relationships
School Science and Mathematics. 2012; 112(5): 278-288. https://doi.
org/10.1111/j.1949-8594.2012.00144.x

Tannen, Deborah. *You Just Don't Understand: Women and Men in*
Conversation HarperCollins. 2013

Taylor, Lynn. *Tame Your Terrible Office Tyrant*
Wiley. 2009

Achor, Sean. *The Happiness Advantage; The Seven Principles of Positive*
Psychology that Fuel Success and Performance at Work
2011

Internet sources

https://www.forbes.com/sites/ekaterinawalter/2014/04/22/4-cs-of-enlightened-leadership/?sh=8dd85fa13456

https://www.forbes.com/sites/janesparrow/2021/02/26/ten-ways-leaders-can-make-their-teams-feel-appreciated/

https://www.michaelpage.com/advice/management-advice/development-and-retention/8-must-have-qualities-effective-leader

https://smallbusinessify.com/the-importance-of-self-confidence-in-leadership/

https://leadinglikeachampion.com/importance-of-accountability-in-leadership/

https://www.citation.co.uk/news/hr-and-employment-law/why-is-staff-training-important/

https://www.michelleray.com/understanding-political-skills-in-great-leaders-office-politics/

https://medium.com/mind-cafe/4-perspectives-all-great-leaders-have-e33d4b23670b

https://leadingwithtrust.com/2016/12/11/too-many-priorities-3-tips-to-focus-on-what-matters-most/

https://vacationtracker.io/blog/the-most-effective-ways-leaders-solve-problems

https://www.linkedin.com/pulse/give-them-problem-solution-kevin-crenshaw

https://www.thnk.org/insights/the-need-for-creative-leadership/

https://www.strategy-business.com/article/Why-leaders-need-a-long-term-view

https://lollydaskal.com/leadership/this-is-why-failure-makes-you-a-better-leader/

https://blogs.illinois.edu/view/8605/1833882347

https://online.hbs.edu/blog/post/importance-of-networking-in-leadership

https://www.forbes.com/sites/yec/2017/10/03/eight-traits-every-powerful-female-leader-possesses/?sh=6e42f0db608f

https://www.replicon.com/blog/17-reasons-women-make-great-leaders/

https://hbr.org/2020/04/7-leadership-lessons-men-can-learn-from-women

https://www.linkedin.com/pulse/women-more-collaborative-men-competitive-david-shindler

https://londonimageinstitute.com/men-women-communication-differences/

https://relationshipsuite.com/4-differences-in-male-and-female-communication-and-how-they-sparks-arguments/

https://online.hbs.edu/blog/post/leadership-communication

https://www.businessnewsdaily.com/1404-characteristics-good-boss.html

https://www.forbes.com/sites/glennllopis/2013/02/18/the-most-successful-leaders-do-15-things-automatically-every-day/?sh=1552de469d7d

https://www.betterup.com/blog/10-core-values-of-a-great-leader

https://www.forbes.com/sites/janesparrow/2021/02/26/ten-ways-leaders-can-make-their-teams-feel-appreciated/?sh=149f9e48aaca

https://www.lollydaskal.com/leadership/its-true-you-cant-do-it-all/

https://www.simplilearn.com/leaders-and-managers-qualities-article

https://www.lollydaskal.com/leadership/why-some-people-are-great-leaders-and-others-are-not/

https://wearethecity.com/the-6-communication-secrets-behind-every-great-woman/

https://real-leaders.com/20-influential-women-share-secrets-leadership-business-life/

https://fairygodboss.com/articles/how-did-she-do-that-4-secrets-of-powerful-women

https://theloop.ecpr.eu/the-secret-of-angela-merkels-extraordinary-success-her-understanding-of-german-politics/

https://www.imf.org/en/News/Articles/2019/08/31/sp083119-Angela-Merkel-Striking-the-Right-Note-on-Leadership

https://www.inc.com/ilan-mochari/time-person-of-year-angela-merkel.html

https://www.theceomagazine.com/business/management-leadership/women-in-leadership-2021/

https://www.cnbc.com/2018/04/10/yum-china-ceo-on-taking-on-career-challenges.html

https://www.theceomagazine.com/business/coverstory/yum-china-joey-wat/

https://www.linkedin.com/pulse/leading-impact-7-leadership-essentials-from-one-fortunes-ellyn-shook

https://www.kiva.org/about/leadership

https://www.businessnewsdaily.com/1404-characteristics-good-boss.html

https://www.roberthalf.jp/en/management-advice/leadership/leader

https://www.nextgeneration.ie/blog/2018/03/the-difference-between-leadership-and-management?source=google.com

https://www.awayre.com/leader-vs-manager-traits-qualities-characteristics/

https://www.businessnewsdaily.com/7481-leadership-quotes.html

https://www.leadershipchallenge.com/research/five-practices.aspx

https://www.flashpointleadership.com/the-five-practices-of-exemplary-leadership

http://www.themuse.com/advice/common-leadership-styles-with-pros-and-cons

https://www.betterup.com/blog/transactional-leadership

https://www.northeastern.edu/graduate/blog/transformational-leadership/

https://www.indeed.com/career-advice/career-development/servant-leadership

https://www.betterup.com/blog/democratic-leadership-style-pros-cons-examples-and-how-to-make-it-work

https://blog.mindvalley.com/autocratic-leadership/

https://www.sortlist.co.uk/blog/bureaucratic-leadership/

https://www.thesuccessfactory.co.uk/blog/laissez-faire-leadership-examples

https://uk.indeed.com/career-advice/career-development/laissez-faire-leadership

https://www.betterup.com/blog/charismatic-leadership

https://www.breathehr.com/en-gb/blog/topic/health-and-wellbeing/8-signs-youre-dealing-with-a-micro-manager-and-how-to-manage-them

https://www.cbsnews.com/news/scientific-proof-that-micro-management-is-bad-for-your-company-and-how-to-fix-it/

https://www.forbes.com/sites/forbescoachescouncil/2018/06/04/try-these-12-strategies-if-you-need-to-stop-micromanaging/?sh=51fb87001c48

https://www.healthguidance.org/entry/13967/1/problem-solving-differences-between-men-and-women.html

https://www.psychologytoday.com/gb/blog/resolution-not-conflict/201202/how-gender-differences-make-decision-making-difficult

https://www.gendereconomy.org/addressing-the-gender-confidence-gap/

https://www.theatlantic.com/magazine/archive/2014/05/the-confidence-gap/359815/

https://www.businessnewsdaily.com/1404-characteristics-good-boss.html

How to train to be a leader

https://www.nextgeneration.ie/blog/2018/03/the-difference-between-leadership-and-management?source=google.com

https://www.entrepreneur.com/article/226265

https://www.strategy-business.com/article/8714

https://www.forbes.com/sites/forbescoachescouncil/2018/02/26/15-biggest-challenges-women-leaders-face-and-how-to-overcome-them/?sh=731bfdd74162

https://www.forbes.com/sites/lizelting/2018/02/28/five-traits-every-woman-leader-needs-to-embrace/?sh=3b02dbc8467f

https://www.nextgeneration.ie/blog/2018/09/high-performing-teams?source=google.com

https://smallbusiness.chron.com/high-turnover-because-recognition-10555.html

https://business.lovetoknow.com/business-operations-corporate-management/motivation-skills-women-vs-men

https://themindspa.co.za/a-look-at-what-motivates-men-and-women/

https://asystems.as/what-drives-us-are-there-gender-differences-motivation-and-values/

https://www.theguardian.com/careers/2016/may/17/the-nine-types-of-employees-and-how-to-motivate-them

https://hbr.org/2021/10/5-things-high-performing-teams-do-differently

http://esheninger.blogspot.com/2018/07/great-leaders-surround-themselves-with.html

https://www.allbusiness.com/behind-every-good-leader-is-a-great-leader-16727574-1.html

https://trainingindustry.com/articles/workforce-development/5-steps-to-build-a-high-performing-team/

https://www.quantumworkplace.com/future-of-work/characteristics-of-high-performing-teams

https://www.simplilearn.com/building-high-performing-teams-article

https://psycnet.apa.org/record/2008-11667-026

https://communicationmgmt.usc.edu/blog/negative-behavior-work-interventions/

https://www.thoughtfulleader.com/leadership-behaviour/

https://www.bamboohr.com/blog/top-bad-leadership-behaviors-how-to-avoid

https://fairygodboss.com/career-topics/bad-behavior-at-work

https://www.thebalancecareers.com/tips-for-minimizing-workplace-negativity-1919384

https://communicationmgmt.usc.edu/blog/negative-behavior-work-interventions/

https://leadchangegroup.com/coaching-employee-change-bad-habit/

https://www.businessnewsdaily.com/8766-resolving-workplace-conflicts.html

https://www.thebalancecareers.com/what-progressive-discipline-1918092

https://blog.procurify.com/2018/02/27/create-manage-budget-implement-better-cost-saving-process/

https://toughnickel.com/business/Manage-Budgets-Understand-the-Purpose-of-Budgets

ttps://toughnickel.com/personal-finance/Manage-Budgets-Understand-How-to-Manage-Budgets

https://blog.procurify.com/2018/02/27/create-manage-budget-implement-better-cost-saving-process/

https://toughnickel.com/business/Manage-Budgets-Understand-How-to-Report-Performance-Against-Budgets

https://www.linkedin.com/pulse/4-essential-budget-management-skills-new-owners-sagar-velagala?trk=public_profile_article_view

https://www.accountingdepartment.com/blog/ten-ways-to-improve-your-budgeting-forcasting

https://aboutleaders.com/time-management-workplace/

https://lucemiconsulting.co.uk/benefits-of-time-management/

https://www.learningarchitects.com/how-time-management-affects-leadership/

https://www.timemanagementtraining.com/time_management_training_Time-Management-Skills-in-Leadership.html

https://www.skillsyouneed.com/rhubarb/manage-time-effectively.html

https://www.lifehack.org/844532/time-management-skills-for-managers

https://www.thoughtfulleader.com/time-management-tips-for-leaders/

http://www.nwlink.com/~donclark/leader/leadtime.html

https://trainingindustry.com/articles/leadership/the-importance-of-time-3-rules-for-effective-leadership/

https://gulfnews.com/world/europe/women-are-better-listeners-study-says-1.1290574

https://www.iberdrola.com/talent/what-is-change-management

https://alignorg.com/the-role-of-leadership-in-change-management/

https://www.forbes.com/sites/forbescommunicationscouncil/2021/11/19/why-change-management-is-the-most-critical-leadership-skill/?sh=444d5b913f22

https://alignorg.com/organizational-design/

https://www.ccl.org/articles/leading-effectively-articles/successful-change-leader/

https://www.ccl.org/articles/leading-effectively-articles/3-steps-for-implementing-change-in-organizations/

https://www.verywellmind.com/imposter-syndrome-and-social-anxiety-disorder-4156469

https://www.stylist.co.uk/entertainment/celebrity/imposter-syndrome-quotes-celebrities/307473

https://stressandanxietycoach.com/quotes-from-9-successful-and-powerful-women-with-imposter-syndrome/

https://www.psichi.org/page/192JNSummer2014#.YvFqbnbMKUk

https://psycnet.apa.org/doiLanding?doi=10.1037%2F0033-3204.30.3.495

https://www.bbc.com/worklife/article/20200724-why-imposter-syndrome-hits-women-and-women-of-colour-harder

https://blog.hubspot.com/marketing/impostor-syndrome-tips

https://info.kpmg.us/news-perspectives/people-culture/kpmg-study-finds-most-female-executives-experience-imposter-syndrome.html

https://womensleadership.kpmg.us/content/womensleadership/en/index.html

https://melodywilding.com/5-fundamental-things-leaders-can-do-to-combat-imposter-syndrome/

https://www.forbes.com/sites/jacquelynsmith/2012/03/06/how-to-be-more-confident-at-work/?sh=19ae35ffd9b2

https://universumglobal.com/blog/why-we-need-to-talk-about-the-confidence-gap/

https://www.ft.com/content/8ea25414-07be-11ea-a958-5e9b7282cbd1

https://zengerfolkman.com/articles/the-confidence-gap-in-men-and-women-how-to-overcome-it/

https://www.kaplanprofessional.edu.au/blog/why-is-confidence-in-the-workplace-important-and-how-do-i-improve-mine/

https://www.linkedin.com/pulse/surprising-secret-greater-confidence-impact-work-mel-robbins

https://susanjeffers.com/2022/07/30/you-dont-have-to-be-alone-with-your-fear/

https://susanjeffers.com/2022/08/10/fear-truths-reviewed/

https://www.adnews.com.au/opinion/feel-the-fear-and-do-it-anyway

https://herleadershipjourney.com/wp-content/uploads/2022/07/3-Steps-to-Become-influential-in-your-workplace-1.pdf

https://www.mindtools.com/pages/article/self-confidence-others.htm

https://www.kellyservices.ca/ca/business-services/business-resource-centre/managing-employees/how-to-boost-employees-confidence/

https://www.forbes.com/sites/paycom/2017/02/03/4-ways-to-build-employee-confidence-and-increase-engagement/?sh=538ff1be1705

https://www.success.com/7-ways-to-build-your-employees-self-confidence/

https://www.pentasia.com/blog/2021/05/how-to-master-negotiation-in-the-workplace?source=google.com

https://techspective.net/2018/10/27/why-leaders-need-to-know-how-to-negotiate/

https://www.forbes.com/sites/forbescoachescouncil/2019/08/06/the-skill-of-workplace-negotiation/?sh=6da7ddf2595f

https://invoicebus.com/blog/leaders-need-negotiation-skills/

https://hbr.org/2018/08/how-women-can-get-what-they-want-in-a-negotiation

https://www.progressivewomensleadership.com/effective-negotiating-why-women-have-an-edge/

https://www.forbes.com/sites/martinrand/2021/03/26/women-have-unique-advantages-as-negotiators-how-can-they-best-leverage-them/?sh=6995fd2d2dac

https://www.forbes.com/sites/forbescoachescouncil/2019/08/06/the-skill-of-workplace-negotiation/?sh=6da7ddf2595f

https://www.pentasia.com/blog/2021/05/how-to-master-negotiation-in-the-workplace?source=google.com

https://techspective.net/2018/10/27/why-leaders-need-to-know-how-to-negotiate/ey.com/en_gl/consulting/how-transformations-with-humans-at-the-center-can-double-your-success

https://www.ey.com/en_gl/workforce/debunking-workforce-mobility-myths

https://www.ey.com/en_gl/workforce/work-reimagined-survey

https://www.pwc.com/gx/en/services/legal/employment/remote-work-for-the-cross-border-workforce.html

https://www.linkedin.com/pulse/quick-guide-lead-employees-cross-countries-ole-philipsen

https://www.ey.com/en_gl/workforce/how-flexible-organizations-can-create-stability-in-the-great-resignation

https://www.forbes.com/sites/carolinecastrillon/2021/12/12/5-ways-to-learn-about-company-culture-before-you-accept-the-job/?sh=7deb4f33d659_

https://hbr.org/2018/01/the-leaders-guide-to-corporate-culture_

https://www.lumapps.com/employee-experience/how-to-build-company-culture/

https://www.thebalancemoney.com/what-is-company-culture-2062000

https://www.biospace.com/article/11-indications-of-a-good-company-culture/

https://www.forbes.com/sites/alankohll/2018/08/14/how-to-build-a-positive-company-culture/?sh=6ef1bdca49b5

https://blog.vantagecircle.com/company-culture/

https://connecteam.com/building-company-culture/

https://blog.bonus.ly/improve-company-culture/

https://www.gra.uk.com/blog/10-tips-for-changing-your-organisations-culture

https://hbr.org/2017/06/changing-company-culture-requires-a-movement-not-a-mandate

https://www.forbes.com/sites/davidrock/2019/05/24/fastest-way-to-change-culture/?sh=14b6b4e23d50

https://www.cipd.co.uk/knowledge/fundamentals/relations/communication/factsheet#gref

https://www.accenture.com/gb-en/insights/strategy/organizational-culture?c=acn_glb_omni-connectedegoogle_13013908&n=psgs_0522&gclid=CjwKCAiAqt-dBhBcEiwATw-ggMElb7hFFg8S2MZoyJRfYUeSmRe-_qbry53J1iYkz5m9yae8dAhXEBoCfFEQAvD_BwE

https://www.sandrazimmer.com/how-i-prepare-professionals-to-interview-for-leadership-positions/

https://career.guru99.com/top-50-leadership-interview-questions/

https://www.inveniaspartners.com/how-prepare-c-suite-executive-interview/

https://www.sandrazimmer.com/how-i-prepare-professionals-to-interview-for-leadership-positions/

https://www.leadershipreview.net/eight-tips-for-your-ceo-job-interview/

Printed in Great Britain
by Amazon

27572770R00093